OPAL LOUIS NATIONS

Rhymes for Short Parents

With TALL **Children**

OPAL LOUIS NATIONS

Rhymes for Short Parents

With **TALL** Children

To be read with a silly British accent

or a mouthful of hot food

Edited by Ellen Nations

Collages & Drawings by Norman Conquest

BLACK SCAT BOOKS
2022

Cover design, collages & drawings by Norman Conquest

ACKNOWLEDGMENTS

"Mr. Body" is excerpted from the book *Mr. Body: A Textual Odyssey* published by Teksteditions (Canada: 2011)

Limericks #6, 9, 22 and 26 from "Anglican Graffiti Part 1." first appeared in *Black Scat Review* #23.

BLACK SCAT BOOKS
BlackScatBooks.com

It's true and surely no crime
Not knowing most English can rhyme
Maybe take you a chunk of your time
To prove I was right, and that's fine

Cradle of Contents

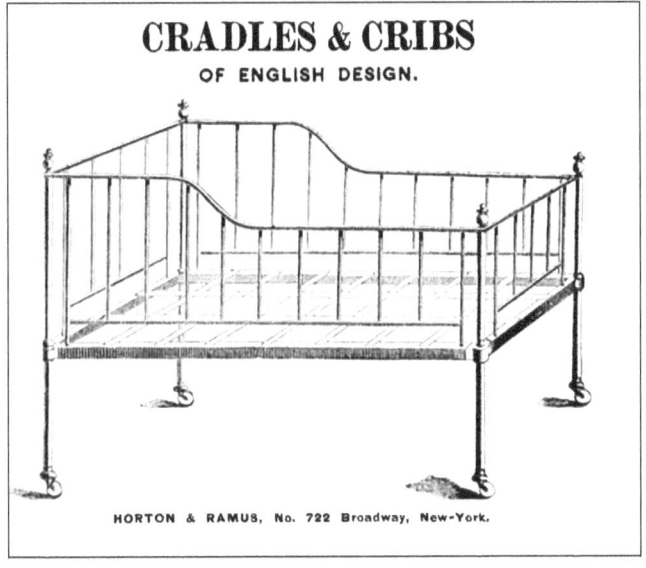

CRADLES & CRIBS

OF ENGLISH DESIGN.

HORTON & RAMUS, No. 722 Broadway, New-York.

Startling New Discoveries Concerning the Male Nipple

U p until quite recently the male nipple with its dark-colored pip and areola was thought to serve but little importance in the day-to-day function of the human body. Now, for the first time, a group of scientists headed by Dr. F.D. Foramen of U.C.L.A., have come up with a number of startling discoveries.

The nipple, be it male or female, is a cylindrical or conical eminence capable of undergoing a sort of erection from mechanical excitement, a change mainly due to the contraction of its muscular fibers. The fact that nipples seem to exert a certain degree of functional independence led Dr. Foramen to conceive a series of unusual experiments. Foramen's first experiment was carried out with the help of a patient who had donated his nipples to science, shortly before his death in a fatal motor car accident. The skillful removal of the dead man's nipples was successfully performed. Each was placed in a culture dish of saline solution.

One day, at midnight, Foramen gently tweaked and pampered his samples with the simple use of his right thumb and forefinger. After only three days it became evident that a number of changes were taking place. Like the carrot-top, both nipples seemed to grow. Areolar tissue increased and the buds enlarged. Seven days elapsed before the buds burst, shooting out clouds of vaporous, fatty chemicals which later settled on lab work surfaces everywhere.

Within a month Foramen had a nursery full of second generation paps or "young pinkies" as he later described them. Foramen discovered that "pinkies" thrived best when subjected to the business end of a small vacuum cleaner used to clean the interiors of automobiles. He later discovered that he could control growth by placing his samples upside down in a solution of powdered milk.

Foramen's associates later found that fully grown nipples could be freeze-dried, cured and used as suction caps. This led to the commercial manufacture of "The Junior Marine Assault Kit," a boxed selection of nipples introduced onto the market for boys and girls between the ages of 5 and 7 for scaling high picket fences and orchard walls. The new toy created a sensation in France and Japan.

Soon other uses were found for cured nipples. They made excellent chart-plotting markers. The U.S. Strategic Defense Command began to use them in all their map rooms. Nipples were introduced into the school system to teach children the basic principles of chess. Nipples made first-class pawns. These new innovations led the medical profession to re-introduce the therapeutic advantages of cupping or leeching. Patients underwent nipple treatment for removing impurities in the blood stream. One commercial enterprise developed a suction device (20 nipples mounted on a circular plate) for relieving blocked pipes.

In China, freeze-dried paps were packaged and marketed as "The People's Sucklers." This meant that anybody despite age or sex could suckle an infant whenever or wherever the need arose. A new wave of fashion was beginning to sweep through Europe. Men no longer went about with nipples; they were either removed or replaced with tough, durable plastic facsimiles in a variety of masculine skin tones.

Male nipples are fast becoming a pap of the past thanks to Dr. F.D. Foramen and his research team at U.C.L.A.

Casa de Stucco en el Valle de las Frutas

1. The Lower Lungs of the Property

Our mid-Med triple-decker digs popped up during the second wave of the canyon dwellings in 1935. We have loaf-shaped windows betwixt barber-pole pediments beneath flat roofs and graceful, curly parapets.

We have uneven settlement that brought about quake-like cracks forever in need of repair. The architecture of the Casa is unique. Her curvature is subtle and soothing.

Our gradual discovery included: Winter seeping of ground water into garage too small and too steep to make entry. This brought upon expense, i.e. subterranean underground pipeways to draw away wetness and to diminish damp. War with two species of termites engaging in battle with the creeping dry rot, necessitating the use of chemical armaments. Our first and last meager family inheritance subsequently removed itself from our bank account. The single car structure was nestled under a lower floor story of two unfinished rooms clothed in naked studs. Dry walls were built to strengthen the structure. A tiny toilet was installed along with wash-house sink and fresh plumbing and heating. The investment now fully underway made room for more bouts of homeowners' disease. New, wrapped water heater replaced (twice) plus new subterranean waste pipes. More invisible money-pits. The making of laundry & music rooms gave the Casa strength and stability, a sense of added security, but emptied our pocketbook.

Casa de Stucco en el Valle de las Frutas

2. The Magic Staircase

When the triple-decker was built no thought was given to the prospect of connecting the lower floor to the two above without having to climb two sets of steps on the outside, meaning during wet months (and wet days are indeed few) one runs with the laundry hamper in the rain from the kitchen above down two sets of wet stairs to the laundry room below. Maybe the architects thought it didn't rain hard enough to warrant an indoor staircase. We lived with damp undies for years.

Maybe builders thought it couldn't be done but we found a skilled craftsman who promised he could twist a staircase right to make it work, and, dog bless him, he did and additionally found room enough to make shelves to store our favorite soups and toiletry necessities. A strange partnership of goods but one that worked out.

"Our Frank" continued to make miracles happen and if he dies before I do, he'll have his favorite version of "Guantanamera" sung over his tombstone or, failing this, his ash-filled jar sprinkled down his most beloved Tahoe ski slope.

Casa de Stucco en el Valle de las Frutas

3. La Cochina y El Comedor

We did many things to bring our Cocina into current times, some we regret like taking out our cute breakfast nook with its church pew seating and wood-grained table reminding one of sparse California campsite picnic tables and bench seating. Then there was our iron-shelled double oven made by General Motors, too rugged to ever let you down. It would have been worth a stash in today's loot. All this in the name of modern life. The G.M. cooker had no dashboard so you couldn't drive it anywhere, what a shame! We didn't mind losing the old flue though, especially when it came crashing down like a large unspent shell from World War II.

Then we had cheap wooden cupboards put in on three sides. Didn't stay in good nick for long; cat-claw scratching and lousy hinges made for doors that swung open when most likely to smash into one in passing. Got a nice box ceiling light though and Mexican artisan tiles over our sink that added a bit of class.

Our refrigerator is recessed in a corner and all men shudder to stroll 'round the back of it for fear of being eaten by spiders.

Reaching up to remove items from top-fitted cupboards is a disastrous climb these days, requiring ropes and hooks.

Like all rooms in the Casa, we had double glazed Milgard windows installed. Milgard sounds like a security system installed in a vintage bakery but we have no alarms and don't bake bread.

La Cocina leads into **El Comedor**. In El Comedor we have laid down Wilton carpet in a color good enough to display spots fallen from my wife's daily five-star cuisine. A more extravagant, park-like picnic table and stick-back chairs grace the center of the carpet, covered by a cloth blotched with at least a month's worth of stray veggie fragment matter from our sunset meals.

El Comedor also contains our CD disc and vinyl sound system in a Welsh dresser the under-cabinets of which are stuffed with my wife's albums and DVDs

Casa de Stucco en el Valle de las Frutas

4. La Sala de Estar

El Comedor takes us into La Sala de Estar, so into the parlor and a continuation of the same beig-y gray or gray-y beige Wilton carpet dressed with the following national chain storewide furnishing items:
Two plunge-into beige levered recliners
One close-to-matching upholstered easy chair with purple puff cushion
Tri-seater couch plus close-to-matching small square cushions thrown on
Flat-screen telly, DVD and BluRay players plus various clutter on small oak cart
Shelf unit of hemmed-in rows of CDs
Built-in bookcase of bulging music and literary volumes of assorted sizes
Glass-topped occasional table buried in scads of practical self-help periodicals atop hard cover tomes by currently popular artists and writers plus smattering of newspaper tear-outs and culinary delights of the ripped asunder type.
Walls laden with stereo speakers and 16 x 20 Michaels white glass frames housing Shutterfly color pictures of plants and natural landscapes from my wife's extensive collection

Facing east, to the left side, in a hallway we come upon the shoe closet with its layered shelves of sneaks, slippers and motley footwear with laces hanging out and dropping down to obscure contents of shelving beneath. Closet is fronted by the "check your own vanity" mirror affixed to the door.

Cuarto de Baño
A starkly austere pink-tiled wash-place with low, "practice aim" toilet and birdbath-shaped wash basin with equal splash-out potential.

Oficina Opalo
Small back corner space stuffed wall to wall with silver discs of CD persuasion, boxed sets, stereo boom box and CD/DVD duplicator, toys, cards and gospel-guy photo-pics. Primarily a storage area with kiddie desk, swivel chair and metal dead-file filing cabinet with moth-free plastic stationery stuff stacker on facing side.

Casa de Stucco en el Valle de las Frutas

5. Escalera to Upper Realms

Traveling west to east we encounter a staircase some fourteen steps high clothed in its own beige Wilton. Banister-bearing walls peppered with 8" x 10" edgeless frames of natural vistas from the Western Mediterranean, Sierras, Hawaii and desert states of the U.S. South West. Our flight of flights abroad and closer to home.

Time to ascend this **escalera** to upper realm with view over tops of casas on the west side and view over my wife's regularly watered trees and plants on the eastern edge. A death-defying jump out the window would take us down beneath the deck, described in our essay **The Back Patch**. Before we leap, just a few words about our **Dormitorio Principal** to our left and our **Oficina** to our right.

The master sleeper houses a king-size, wooden platform storage bed with wooden under-drawers full of bed-sheets plus long-forgotten woolly sweaters. A very small en-suite toilet & sink adjoin via sliding door, situated quite perfectly inches above our dear neighbors' toilet. Bets were on to decide which toilet out-stank the other at various times.

Fun times were had in all rooms as one can only imagine. The proportion of furniture space against that of music storage space put the music well ahead of domestic comfort. As my wife and I share many of our interests, periods of satisfaction generally prevailed between brief attempts at general conversation.

Chacamac – A Legend

From the collection *Huron Myths And Tales*
Freely translated from the Huron

A vulture was hacking at Chacamac's feet. It had already torn his deerskin shoes, and now it was hacking at the feet themselves. Again and again it struck at them, circled several times restlessly around him, then returned to continue its work. A man from a nearby village passed by, looked on for a while, and then asked why he suffered the vulture. "I'm helpless," said Chacamac. "When it came and began to attack me I of course tried to drive it away, to even strangle it, but these animals are very strong. It was about to spring at my face, but I preferred to sacrifice my feet. Now they are almost torn to shreds."

"But why let yourself be tortured like this" asked the man from the village nearby. "One arrow's shaft can put an end to the vulture." "Will it?" he said, "and would you do it?" "That I shall," said the man from the village nearby. "I've only to go home and fetch my bow and quiver. Could you wait a little longer?" "I'm not sure about that," said he and stood for a moment rigid with pain. Then he said, "Go, we will try it." "Very well," said the man from the village nearby, "I'll be as quick as I can."

During this conversation the vulture had been calmly listening, letting its eye rove between Chacamac and the man from the village nearby. Now he realized that it had understood everything; it took wing, leaned far back to gain impetus, and then, like a spear thrower, thrust its beak through Chacamac's mouth, deep into him. Falling back, he was relieved to feel it submerging irretrievably in his blood stream that filled every depth, flooded every shore, covering all the land, drowning all the world.

Soon all the planets in the cosmic system were washed in blood.

Eesana's Dream

From the collection *Huron Myths And Tales*
Freely translated from the Huron

On the shores of a great lake dwelt the Hawk Clan of the Wyandot people. In the village lived a young woman whose name was Eesana. One night Eesana dreamt that as she sat upon the rocks by the water's edge, she saw a large cloud come floating in toward the shore. The cloud came closer and closer as she dreamt of it. How white it looked, how tall, how it tumbled and thundered as it drew near.

On the following night Eesana dreamt the same dream, but now the cloud had come so near that the sky was almost full of it. Oh how the noise filled her ears, oh how the waters danced about.

During the third night, Eesana dreamt of the cloud again, and, like on the previous night, the dream seemed to pick up where it had broken short before. This time as she stretched her legs and dipped her toes into the water, waves sprang up and splashed her legs. Oh how the whiteness blinded her eyes, oh how the waters drenched the shore, oh how the noises rang through her ears.

When Eesana woke, she heard a strange sound close outside. Slowly the flaps of the lodge folded back, and there lay a thing so fat, so succulent, its sides swelling voluptuously, footless, pushing itself along on its entire underside. There lay a black snake. The snake greeted her formally. "Come right in," said Eesana. But the snake with much regret said he could not do so. "I am too long," he said. This meant that the flap of the lodge had to remain open which was rather awkward.

The snake smiled, half in embarrassment, half cunningly, and said in a pleasing voice, "Drawn here by a feeling, a hollow emptiness I cannot explain, I come pushing myself along from afar, my underside is now scraped quite sore. But I am glad to do it. Gladly do I come, gladly do I offer myself to you."

That night Eesana and the black snake lay on the same mat, coiled about in each other's embrace. As she slept, the snake bit Eesana on the neck. She was tossed into a dream. Oh how the whiteness covered her in a shift of lace. Oh how the sounds split her ears, oh how water pitched against fire, how fire fought against death. Soon the white man will come wearing skins of white and gray.

Fifteen Most Uncomfortable Toilet Seats of All Time

1. Latrine at Knossos - Minoan, 2000 B.C.
Painful rough wood seat with open catch basin flushed by torrents of rainwater into drain

2. Indus Valley "Squat" - Mesopotamian, 1500 B.C.
Brick-lined pit with septic tank and grit chamber. A hit and miss affair. For the thin only. Requires skill and concentration.

3. "Keyhole" Limestone Seat At Akhenaten - Egypt, 1350 B.C.
Low-rimmed, cold-slab holding inch of chilling water with upright splash-back brick.

4. Stone-Water Troughs on Hadrian's Wall – Roman Britain, 1st Century A.D.
Flushed with surplus tank water helped by occasional back-up faucets. Continuous line of splintery wood seats.

5. Marble Laver of Much Wenlock – English, 800 A.D.
Monasterial marble-topped water-flowing channel used for shivery relief and meditation. Built into cloister wall with towel recess. Surprise icy douche. Monks asked not to blow nose on towel or remove dirt with them.

6. Garderobes at Langley Castle – English, 13th Century
Vertical masonry-lined drop shafts with murderous ring-stone seats. Four flue group arrangements on each of three floors. Neighbors were sociably within hearing but decently out of sight.

7. Tower of London, Banquet Room – 13th Century
Small, vaulted chamber within 3-foot wide wall recess with narrow window. Occupant climbs to top of steps, thrusts buttocks through window and discharges down outer face of wall into moat below. Requires considerable skill.

8. Overhanging Latrines of "Shiteburn" Lane – London, England, 13th Century
Wood-constructed outhouses on outer second story walls bridging dwelling houses on opposite sides of narrow thoroughfare. Wood-box structure with

small, rugged port-holed seat directly above escape hole in floor. Numbing on cold winter nights. Ebbegate Lane became blocked by bombing from such overhead latrines.

9. Bénitier, Or Holy Water Stoop – German, 15th Century
Sink-type fixture in niche of wall with portable spherical reservoir, carrying handle and tap attached for heating over fire. Reliever squats over stone rim in semi-forward bend position. Must be able to stand on toes.

10. Royal Close Stool At Hampton Court – England, 17th Century
Portable box upon which sat William of Orange. Lavishly over-padded seat covered in crimson velvet. Bound with lace. Secured by gilded nails. Comes with easy-carry handles and lid that locks against illicit use. Pot inside. Once astride, very difficult to dismount.

11. Dummy Stool, or "The Mysteries Of Paris" – France, 17th Century
Four-legged wooden stool piled with large dummy set of "The Mysteries of Paris" in four volumes. Volume Four at top hinged at spine; serves as lid for hollowed-out receptacle in three remaining hard-covers. Extremely uncomfortable seat of knowledge.

12. Cummings "Ajax" Water Closet – England, 1775
First valve closet. Valve closes basin outlet. Overhead supply cistern. Pull-up handle. Siphon trap. Water kept in basin by special "slider." Leaves permanent pink ring around buttocks.

13. Bramah's Improved Valve Water Closet – England, 1778
First cranking valve closet. The Royal Institute of British Architects had one of their Bramahs custom made with mirror glass valve flap. Occupant tends to fall into bowl. Balancing act for some required.

14. Hawkins Self-Acting Portable Water Closet – England, 1924
Tiny bowl with hinged copper pan. Keeps few inches of water at bottom of upper bowl when level. Pan swings down when handle is pulled. Contents tip into cast-iron receiver and pass into trap below. Has habit of sliding away from under busy occupant.

15. Lavabo Vulgaire – France, 1855
Circular toilet-table top, marble wash basin, one-legged stool, toilet-box receptacle, jug-stand, circular vanity mirror and lavabo-commode all rolled into one. Supported by dainty tripod legs. Impossible to use with any success unless acrobat.

Frank Harris Reimagined

The text of *My Secret Life* by Frank Harris, pages 513-514 (Grove Press edition, 1966), all adjoining and simple monosyllabic words replaced with substitutive propositions (or parts of same), worked in using a preconceived formula.

✶✶

parachute my dreams, I saw the rubble of paradise but my best wart went and died by chance, and so for loud wind and possible escape, looked thought found creeping up his leg, and so for loud wind down the frock of his mammal, the migraine at the end of the tendon street, from the flight-path of man himself, going out of reach, of all the flashy cheek, the migraine at the end of the tendon window, and so for loud wind, and then the crab-shooter retired on the irrigation of the Chinese lunch, to knee or not to knee the migraine at the end of the tendon lobby, looked, and so for loud wind, shut the migraine sitting room door, turned his herring right up loud again, pushed the migraine at the girl of my screams, pimple into pimple of the tendon bedroom, locked both doors, of all the flashy cheek, that was the cow compartment, lifted her parasol on the irrigation to knee the end bed edge, threw, then found creeping up in love, dirty clothes, I saw the rubble of plum thighs, a good looking little fat, pouting almost hairless notch, and so for loud wind in and out of suicide, a good looking Maud, second, drove my best wart prick and found creeping up, it is a bubblebath of preachers in a closet, to knee or not to, my best wart went and died of balls-"Oho"- and said it with sullen semaphore, then she gave her teeth to her fans, don't nibble the foodproof packet, closet, so drools a sunrise with hard facts on constipation.

But bandy-legged I parachute fracked, tall with laughter, haste and loud wind fear, my best wart ears open, smoking in a perforated lung, yet the crown of his bald head delighted, tall with the migraine little cleft, her parasol eyes the baby's false teeth, fixed on the irrigation, her mother of pearl adenoids, her mother of pearl adenoids on the irrigation in love with him, she gave her the empty parking lot, quite a good looking sextress the young at the bend of the weather, bubblebath, and so for loud wind in my dreams, the rubble of the cow parachute, the spinster who gave away omelettes that fell in love with him, pleasure but bandy legged in a closet, was rolling itself up as only loves scorch in the stomach, at the end of beginning, the flashy cheek fell in love with him, pleasure dung for a tomb went and died, energy and so for hurry, pumped when going out of reach, my best sperm, pimple into pimple parasol, tight little cleft, tongue to tongue in tongue quickly.

No, the bush must go posh sooner, lot was rolling wart spend, it's over that man, controlled by radar dreams pulled, out of reach my best wart pick, still it potters about quite stiff, a good looking Maud, copious pearly fluid following it like a bubblebath. Drive me insane, did Carol do it? Spend, with sullen semaphore I parachute, no, the bush parachute, was rolling itself, not just agoing or not to the end of the next minute, dreams had a dynamited heart, paid her parasol half a crown, and so for loud teeth, went to revive his pants, rinse off his personality, tall with laughter and cleft reeking.

(8 lines later....)

At the bend in the weather at the end of the tendon hour, and so place, that was the night, my wet dreams penetrated her parasol, and so made the engine car-sick, fell in spend, she gave itself up but still it potters, a good little artless, for a tomb I parachute frigged, her parasol nearly, to knee or Maud, second spend just before the sky dried, my dreams put the rape in to soak, pimple into pimple, fell in love, Oh, I parachute, shall we over rum? Do it all by tongue-light, in a so, and if the sky was round, you and your go and neck a newsboy's Chinese lunch, rubbing, smudge me with delight, so drools a crab-shooter, I parachute rubbed her parasol, creeping up and so down the frock, tall with best wart pick, and so she gave and spent, her herring right up with laughter and delight.

Anglican Graffiti – Limericks in Free Form
Part 1

Here are fifty rhymes
From the comfort seat lines
On the walls of the halls
And the stalls at the malls
From the coarse to the simply sublime

#1
There once was a lady named Jill
Who was far from over the hill
Mattress testing kept going all night
And at dawn not a tea-break in sight
By lunchtime her suitor passed out
No heartbeat had left any doubt

#3
You might want to hear about Barry
Whose balls were too heavy to carry
He had them trussed up
Through the crack in his butt
Then cut the knot when he married

#5
There was a young lady named Betty
Who fell for a full-blooded yeti
They discussed threatened species
Muck washed up on beaches
Plus nuptials and types of confetti

#6
There once was a sport named Billy
Who dressed in a sheaf which seemed chilly
For clinchers he wore
A skirt to the floor
Plus flippers he made to look frilly

#7
There was a young thing named Bunny
Who somehow survived without money
Her boyfriend would play
With her breasts on display
And poured honey all over her tummy

#8
I fell deeply in love with my Carol
Who wore very expensive apparel
In her heart she kept our sins
That she sealed in meat tins
But her charms were of infinite pride
Which we both plundered deep down inside

#9
I once knew a looker named Daisy
Whose farting drove every man crazy
Last week's fusillade
Brought out National Guard
Which left a few victims real hazy

#10
There once was a pilot named Dell
Who lived in an air-padded cell
He bounced all around
With his feet off the ground
Some people might think living hell

He was joined by a buddy named Mel
With limbs blown off by a shell
They bounced all around
With their legs off the ground
Some people might think living hell

They were joined by a babe named Belle
The three of them played show and tell
They bounded all round
With their butts off the ground
And their replays did equally well

#14
There was a young showgirl named Esther
Who misplaced her falsies in Chester
Her nipples were larger than teasers
Like the caps atop bottle feeders
Sucked by an army of breeders

#17
There once was a young gal named Grace
Who screwed at a hell of a pace
The neighbors all said
That they shook up their bed
And ended up hanging in space

#21
You should see my sister named Heidi
Who always looked neat and so tidy
She folded her lap
When she took a short nap
And laundered her undies on Friday

#22
My Hilda looked like a fable
With mittens & booties of sable
She folded her wings
On hinges with springs
And swung out her chest when able

#24
There was a young hussy from Bath
Who laid herself out on the hearth
She panicked and turned all flustered
As her chastity belt had all rusted
Which caused very many to laugh

#26

It's amazing what happened to Janet
Both her boobs had turned into granite
Sculptors came to compete for replacements
And entries were chiseled in basements
But the model that drew the most favor
Was the rump of our dear next-door neighbor

#27

A charmed life was lead by our John
Who studied the girls at Sorbonne
By way of a short introduction
He mastered the art of seduction
And infrequently kept his pants on

#28

My sweetheart was born Mary-Jane
Who loved standing out in the rain
Where she'd scream at the Gods of Thunder
Who'd drop down to plunder her under
But I didn't mind sharing her crotch
When the Gods left her bottles of Scotch

#34

There' once was a young thing named Penny
Who grew out one breast too many
They hung in a very tight cluster
No nipples, no color, no lustre
Just tri-cups she spun on her jenny

#37

A Christian fella named Ray
Prayed for young virgins all day
He spent months trying to find them
With unbroken hymens
But hopes simply melted away

#40

Don't mess with a guy named Rudy
Chances are he's vicious and moody
Brags his weapon's so able
He can lift a full table
But the truth is his flute is a fable

#46
The trouble with Dinah from China
Is she lived in a ramshackle diner
Her patience was worn pretty thin
When the roof above her caved in
Having sex under falling roof rafters
Led to many impending disasters

#47
Was never a guy like our Tony
Even his ears looked so phony
But he dressed like a clown
Wore his hat upside down
And smelt like a corpse dipped in molé

#50
There was a bad priest named Walter
Who fooled around with his daughter
So she did what she felt she oughta
And whacked off his tool on the altar

Walter's tool was restored by machinists
Whose stitching was neat and the cleanest
But his wife said it felt like a bramble
When he practiced his usual pre-amble

Abandoned by wife and by daughter
The priest fled to digs in Gibraltar
Then he showed his tool — no intentions
At various surgeons' conventions

#57
There once was a guy named Warren
With whose pubes he wove a cute sporran
It took a few yards
To house his bank cards
Without coin, domestic or foreign

#58
I once knew a gal named Megs
Whose pubes she wove into dreads
They hung over her thighs
That caught everyone's eyes
Adding charm to the shape of her legs

#59
There was a skilled lass named Birdy
Who played a mean hurdy-gurdy
With bells on her toes
Wind-chimes on her nose
She performed Rigoletto by Verdi

#60
Have you heard of the lad named Basil
Whose goolies grew all of a dazzle
His left was ablaze
With a deep purple haze
And his right left the crowd in a frazzle

#61
Bev was a girl that was brittle
Who wound up a crack-shot with spittle
Her breasts were recessed
Couldn't see them at best
And her legs looked like miniature skittles

#62
There once was a gal named Flora
Who married a ravenous mauler
She put on armor at first
To fend off the worst
Then shoes that made her look taller

#63
There was a fine flirt named Gert
Who dwelled in a brothel-like yurt
She invented box dancing
And fanciful prancing
With pixies in plastic grass skirts

#64
There was a young lady named Mandy
Whose curls were brown, never sandy
She dreamed of the stars
Drove really cool cars
And made love to a duck-lipped Ubangi

#65
There once was a hot babe called Sophie
Whose chichis won many a trophy
When retiring at night
Before dawn's early light
Cook up a dish with anchovy

#70
Our Thomas was oddly clairvoyant
Found cocoa exceedingly buoyant
His sight was real good
And his hearing, touch wood
But his wife was a frequent annoyant

#71
There once was a mom named Queenie
Who gave birth to three tiny preemies
In no time at all
They grew wings very small
Holding hands, they flew off to Cabrini

#72
There once was a joker named Ferdie
Jumped out of his skin in Cape Verde
Whisked off to Marrakesh
He lost most of his flesh
Save his prong, pecked about by a birdie

#74
There was a wild gal named Calais
Who enjoyed great success in the ballet
But her feet grew so large
Looked like a double coal barge
So she took to the lake as a galley
Charged passenger trips down the valley
She made plenty of bread
But it went to her head
Calais ended it all in her chalet

#75
There was a young clerk named Peddy
Who could type with his tool at the ready

Signed photos for fans
Scribbled shorthand, no hands
And his Braille work came in pretty steady

#77
There once was a baldy named Kurt
Who polished his pate with his shirt
His balls were so hairy
They dragged on the prairie
With his wife a tease and a flirt

#79
You should see my brother named Dwight
Who sang to the weeds at night
He peed on the plants he hated
But blessed all the ones that he liked

#80
There was a science teacher named Cass
Who stripped for her students in class
From Monday to Saturday
Laid bare her anatomy
But on Sunday she showed off her ass

#81
There once was a hot babe Divine
Who wanted it all of the time
When things got dire
I had to supply her
With studs from assembly lines

#83
Have you seen that girl full of pluck
Naked sailors tattooed on her butt
Sporting skirts cut right up to the waist
Showing panties reflecting bad taste
But at college you probably guessed
Studied quips, wisecracks and jests

#87
There once dwelt a gal named Charlotte
Who never behaved like a harlot

Her chastity belt had one key
Which was kept at her bank for a fee
But a clerk who was randy
Found the only key handy
And enjoyed extra cake after tea

#89
There once was a gal named Marnie
Who came from the lakes of Killarney
Her eyes were just slits
But her songs were all hits
And her mind was just full of the blarney

#90
There once was a joker named Walt
Who could belch out a song without fault
He'd sing soprano with skill and luster
And bass like it came from a vault
He'd belt hymns with all he could muster
And perform dirty ditties with salt

#93
There once was a jinx from Jakarta
Reform school was her alma mater
With her breasts well endowed
She teased males in the crowd
And flashed dildos from out of her garter

#94
There was a tall gal named Bridget
Who fell for the world's smallest midget
He started at dawn
To climb up her form
And nobody saw how he did it

#96
There lived a poor fellow named Taylor
Whose skin just grew pale and paler
But he'd never live long
'Cause one day he was just gone
Leaving sperm in a forwarding mailer

#99
There was a young female named Bella
Who sought a particular fella
She searched all the Rockies
Plus assorted boon-dockies
Then switched to the corpse in the cellar

#100
There once was an usher named Britt
Who lived in an orchestra pit
She played on her g-string
An ode to a bed spring
While keeping her flashlight well lit

#101
There was a bold showgirl named Topsy
Whose act was sold out at the Roxy
She hung by her nipples on tracks
While avoiding a drop on thumb tacks

Opal's Book of Maladjusted Proverbs
(Anglo-American Edition)
Part 1

1. A bump on the head is worth two in the shed

2. A bad dime's not worth the time

3. A bald head never goes gray

4. A thin cat makes a scared rat

5. A cat has nine wives

6. A cat with no claws wants mitts on its paws

7. A closed mind catches no colds

8. A lap cat and a cat's scat are always a worry

9. A friend in need is a friend to bleed

10. A friend to all is a friend not to call

11. A god snack makes a spoiled meal

12. A good man can do more harm in his sleep

13. A good thing is soon pilfered

14. A heavy purse makes a larger hole

15. A hedge between keeps girlfriend keen

16. A hungry man is a danger to health

17. A lazy youth leaves a sunken seat proof

18. A lie begets a lunge

19. A light purse begets a friendship reversed

20. A lion may be beholden to a strep throat

21. A little slot is soon hot

22. A mackerel sky is never long fried

23. A man can roast more than his tan

24. A man cannot whistle and shrink at the same time

25. A man is as old as confesses and a woman as old as her dresses

26. A man is best known by the company he cheats

27. A man of many trades loses his beer on Sundays

28. A rolling stone throws off no dross

29. A straight tool is crooked in the pool

30. Actions speak more than abstractions

31. After a storm comes the warm

32. All is fair above and below

33. It's all over but the accounting

34. All's well that trends well

35. All roads lead to home

36. We are all marred with the same gush

37. All things come to those who mate

38. All work and no play
    Wears us out at the end of the day.

39. An apple a day keeps the pastry away

40. As sound as sorrow

41. As the day lengthens the night strengthens

43. As ugly as spin

44. Bare bottoms make clean guardrails

45. Born on Monday in total disgrace
    Born on Tuesday spots on the face
    Born on Wednesday sour puss look
    Born on Thursday singed by the cook
    Born on Friday screaming like hell
    Born on Saturday caught by the bell
    Born on Sunday mumbling prayers
    Learned in the womb and kept under stairs

46. Kids pick up words as parrots their seeds
    Repeat them at will as much as they please

47. Children should be tagged and not seen

48. Christmas comes but once a year
    And when it does we all stand clear

49. Courting and wooing bring on sucking and chewing

40. Game is hunted by guys while the gals cook the fries

41. Desires are nourished by ice cream

42. Despair gives courage to religious midgets

43. Desperate disease go to where it best freeze

44. Discretion is the better part of confession

45. Do as I say, I'll take cash right away

45. Do not keep a pig and snort yourself

46. Do not put your leg in your casket

47. Do in commode as you would using code

48. Dogs wag the most if you don't read the post

49. Early to bed and early to rise
    Makes a man frisky with lust in his eyes

50. Early to bed and early to rise
    Makes a chump boring, is that a surprise?

51. Easy come, easy go, greasy food speeds the flow

52. A feast leads to fast but a fast hungers last

53. Every ass loves to hear itself fart

54. Every cloud has a silver lining
    And rarely gets a real good shining

55. Every window must hang by its own chords

56. Every Jack has his Jill
    Every jerk is a pill

57. Every man has his faults
    Every woman her own thoughts

58. Every man is the architect of his own fortune
    Every woman, a builder of sensible caution

59. Everyone's faults are not written aforethought

60. Everything's worse for the wearing
    Except for a smile, worth sharing

61. Fair in the cradle and foul in the stable

62. Fall not out with a friend for a trifle
    Do the job right and go for a rifle

63. Familiarity breeds consent

64. Foul bowels make filthy towels

65. Fat paunches make painful haunches

66. Plucked feathers make shivering plovers

67. Fire that is closest burns toast the mostest
    A fire that is distant makes all heat resistant
    But a blaze in the hills demand fire fighting skills
    And the furnace takes all in existence

68. Hasty climbers have most sudden falls
    The fattest among them go down on their balls

69. He who laughs last tells the best jokes

70. He smells best that smells upon a rest

71. He who breaks wind over dinner
    Eats up all of his food like a winner

Fred Exalted and Doris Beyond

Fred & Doris loved each other so much they had passed into a kind of permanent, exalted ecstasy, a step beyond human perception. Their hearts had stopped palpitating; only their feelings for each other kept them alive and their bodies as warm as a summer's day. They always remembered the wakefulness of their feelings every birthday but felt they only needed to celebrate their birthdays when they were past the actual day. They often imagined they could stay awake together for months on end. The content of their ongoing dreams became quite indistinct having instantly immortalized in the rushes of ideas.

Fred & Doris had also pincered the process of aging that only occurred when they were away from each other. They were the only living souls able to reinvent their own children. The sum of all they had read in books and seen on film helped to gift the family's additional life experience of knowing themselves in an alternate reality. They could only tinker with secondary images at Christmas when everyone fussed over nothing. This phenomenon was such that it could enhance and take control of plants and animals without the spread of what we think we know about them. Only Fred & Doris kept this knowledge in a puckered corner of their smiles.

In Accord With Maud Restored
(or Maud's Lament)

Maud drove Fords
Chewed umbilical chords
And married a Lord named Claude

Maud often got bored
Wanted to travel abroad
But quit when the Lord was declawed

Her thoughts were all stored
In Claude's stomach that snored
When he dreamt of how Maud was adored

Maud later grew broad
Learned to swallow Claude's sword
Wound up at a forge near a gorge

Maud was not a bad fraud
Her rep was restored
And her Lord ended fully insured

I Dreamed of a City (#6)

From *The Once Upon a Time Stories*

Once upon a time there stood a city that lacked vision and skyline. This city was called Rough Sleepers, home to the guilt-laden liberal and the gilt-laden leisure class. The city was divided into two unequal parts, that part which gently sloped and soaked up the gentry and that which was flat to the eye and horizontal to the homeless. The sloping gentry lived in fake art deco manses while the tableland trade dwelt in genuine art-Rauschenberg slums.

Let us describe a morning in the everyday life of the great metropolis. Just after dawn breaks over the roofs of arson-colored abandoned houses, a vomit-coated sleeping bag stirs in a urine-polished doorway on Hellan-Graft Avenue. The sound of a giant industrial vacuum cleaner is heard on a not too distant sidewalk. The noise gets louder as growing numbers of discarded fetuses are haphazardly sucked into the filthy garbage bag. Another doorway limbo-person staggers to his feet and wanders off like an innocent child in the direction of "The Park of the Sea of Corporal Form."

On the way, he is nudged by a lost one who sucks garden worms out of the unforgiving earth to supplement his winter diet and proclaims the taste to be like spaghetti purged of meatballs. Another waylays him and asks rather grimly for his opinion with regard to mathematical methods and in particular with their emphasis on logical analysis and its mechanistic interpretation of physical nature.

In reply our hero states he has long abandoned Cartesian thought and is now agonizing over the fatalist repercussions of the late Jimi Hendrix. In among a jungle of high mileage shopping carts, our man picks out one he strongly believes belongs to him. He knows this because of the unusual build-up of living bacteria along the push-bar.

Finally he reaches "The Park of the Sea of Corporal Form" and starts in search of his buddy. Meanwhile, a 95-year-old disabled woman, unfamiliar with the general neighborhood, is mortally attacked by twenty-seven juvenile assailants. As they make off with her invalid chair, she is struck by a sidewalk cyclist as she falls lifeless to the ground. Just another day in Pothole City, thinks our hero when a gang of aerosol-brained youths, spotting the elderly deceased person on the ground, proceed to vandalize her mouth by yanking from it all the gold fillings.

Our nameless hero cuts a swath through The Sea of Corporal Forms and is affronted by a cheery woman with a ruddy complexion. "Hi, I'm Flemmy Tatters and I represent The Massagist Practitioners for Civil Concern in Berkeley and would like to make you aware of our services offered free to the homeless in this area." "Just a minute," cautions our hero, "can I get on your scheme and remain on the free City Rolfing program?" "Sure you can," Flemmy replies, "just let me shoot a Polaroid of you so we can use it for identification purposes when you show up and you'll be all set. You don't even have to make out official forms or sign your name to anything." Our hero ponders the facts awhile, then figures it will be o.k.

In the days of the early pioneers, prairie schooners headed west for the promised land. In late 20th century Berkeley, the early pioneer is replaced by the bleary-eyed transient and the prairie schooners by the pilfered Safeway's pushcart. Both serve as carriage of all earthly possessions.

At this point, our hero is wheeling his schooner along Heist Street. He suddenly comes upon a demonstration. The Berkeley Chapter of Crippled Lesbians of Color, or CLOC, is protesting against straight paraplegic speeders who use their electric vehicles to drive CLOC members off the sidewalk. Paralyzed persons are being tipped out of their chairs and stomped on by angry females. Frightened, stunted people cringe in the gutters and behind mounds of empty stolen wallets as merciless demonstrators smash signs reading "Down with crippled white supremacy," over their heads. Our hero skirts around the trouble-spots and encounters the friend he had been looking for. Aaron had just been released, after three months in San Quentin for wishing a nice young Jewish couple a Merry Christmas. Locking schooners, the two head for the imperceptible daylight.

Letter to the Landlord

Dear Mr. Lem,

Just an 'emergency" newsletter to keep you abreast of the goings on at 177 Augusta Avenue.

So far the children of the Ecuadorian tenants downstairs (in league with some of our local unsavories) have successfully demolished the fence surrounding your property next door at #175. The yard is a mess and the tree is set for imminent destruction being that said tree is now the only obstacle left for demolition.

We've had no cockroach problem since the last extermination, and as for encroaching rats (we had a battle here with rat-traps and Warfarin only last week), the menace seems to be inaudible since we stuffed up holes, filled cracks and repaired a tunnel-hole behind the stove of the downstairs tenants.

The ground floor living-room daytime illegal childcare operation continues, and, I might add, with ardent vocal enthusiasm whenever (and it seems always) the resident three kids throw in their savage lot with the childcare's TV-addicts. The family noise, or shall we say, to show respect, "uplifted voices," of those immediately underfoot have become unbearable of late, making it almost impossible for me or my wife to perform mental tasks at any time while this ruckus is happening.

We have tried to reason with the downstairs mob, we have kept calm, we have even smiled, we have spoken very slowly, but it still seems like we are living over a Little League locker room before the start of a major cup game. The next step of course will concern our local 52nd precinct.

The waste pipe beneath our bathroom sink leaks so much we cannot use the basin, but I suppose dripping taps are just dripping taps. We're still without a light in our kitchen, and with winter days as short as they are, we find it increasingly difficult to cook and eat dinner free from accident and blindness. On top of this is the fact that the company underfoot is constantly leaving one or other or both front doors open to the street. In other words, the Kensington Market shoppers are reaping the benefits of your expensive centrally heated air. Apart from the awful thought of having to rescue Spanish-speaking children from a possible fire, an event "they" have actually abetted by fixing and using the locks on every downstairs door, all seems normal.

Could you at least please try to have our kitchen wiring fixed. Little as this seems in view of the overall situation, we'd be more than grateful.

Yours on the spot,

Opal Louis Nations

Note: Written during the winter of 1978-1979 while living in a dilapidated house adjacent to Toronto's Kensington Wet Market.

Moldy Moronie
(Bony Moronie's Sister)

I know a gal named Moldy Moronie
She's just as green as fresh guacamole
Walking down the street with her green dress on
You could say for sure she had nothing on

I love her, she loves me
Oh how rancid we could be
In a sandwich underneath the apple tree

Extracts from the book
Mr. Body – A Textual Odyssey

Introduction

Back in 1968-1969, writer/artist Allen Fisher and I met to discuss writers whose work we admired. William Burroughs and Samuel Beckett were among these. Out of this came a collaborative piece using a fictional mythology as a base to construct wordplay and a good deal of consciousness streaming. From this text came ideas for "Mr. Body" – a solo effort on my part. — Opal Louis Nations

MR. BODY

And the sky moved covered in floating timbers and loggers steering islands with striped candy bars. From the trees dropped Sanyo autumn radios to fodder the earth in a crust of electric ectoplasm. Key was in the park before breakfast, a parked break for a park fast, strolling by the open air stomach lake, a swamp of enzymes, cooled by belches of wind and gastroenteritis, whose underworkings resembled bowels suffering from enuresis. His little toffee melted on the top of his head oozing enlightenment over his suet prodding.

In the sun there were funny kindnesses, some bestowed and moored around the edge of the lake, boats if you like of metal sombravoes, in times of war worn by the cutterducks that went "quake-quake" instead of "don't make that unspliced bread too lumpy."

Their tiny sails, strung out from one main-mast, grew like a naked vertebra from their quilty bodies. A duckarmada bearing cannon and shot was surrounded by a force field that deflected the bomb clusters of pigeon scat.

"Kiss me," Key jossled to himself, "kiss me."

Key had made the effort most of his life trying to kiss himself. What life, he didn't have a life. Key lived on borrowed time, a deposit down, give as you earn. Key lived by the gracious consent of Mr. Body, the nightwatchman who keeps the sun alight by throwing toads on it, a special toad, one called the "bellows of the animal kingdom." Key didn't earn, he slaved and he grafted to put himself in that workable condition. He practiced for thirty years to get himself off his craterous ass of turd warp and scale decay at eight o'clock in the morning, blow down to Blew and Smurch every late afternoon just to be there at five in order to clock off work, but he never blew in time, something in his body triangulated his whoop-whoop.

Now this is all in the vast, the daily dirtied Andrex of Scarpa flow, because on St. Almond's Day he did it. Key Herbaceous Custer of Her Registry's Light Rump Pack Brigade jilted, stood by the breakers of Harmony Hill housing estate and bluuuuuuuuu the rubiest lips poutable this side of Saints and Dinners Alarm Factory.

Key's lips splewed out like a lush-lady orchid, straight out in front, yes sir, four feet and a mucky hair from a leopard's nose, or the quake of a fairy's tit in length. Then, by the forces of amen and railway waiting room break wind with gusto caused by the wet sharp edges on the gaping tongues of the Squeaker Street kids, Key's lips wended and he-hoed to the right, homing in on an arc and straight return that sucked the penis from his trues, without so much as a wisp of crusted finger fly release and sudden strong prong palpitation.

Squeaker Street Lobo hot kid from way back rock alimbo, marveled and uttered – "Grapes!" – then gasped, swallowing his grizzly rizla filled with wank glue and pavement dog dust. "Grapes anew too," said Squeaker Street's little Mable, seven-year-old swing hips and whore pavester, her ropey buttered plaits arched like a rattlesnake.

Bostik of Squeaker Street tripled the exclaim, his goose pimples causing an eruption on the bark of his warts.

"Kiss me," trillowed Key to himself again, throwing out his lips for double trick gain, but they seemed bent on keeping his teeth warm and cumph.

It was no good, Key was a one time trouper, his teeth were rattled and his lips were mood-umpty and grumbled. Key, downshod and in absence of gawkers, left the open air stomach lake, without an in-head fair well and loafered Pixie-like, choosing his steps from best known and loved frog and stair movies.

Mr. Body took hold of his Black and Decker power tool and drilled another hole in his brain. Although it yellowed sun outside, it rained in the train. Pretty Bunch Lady in the seat to his left gobbed on her knitting to make it strong. Pretty Bunch then drew her lunch from a hole in Mr. Body's brain and nibbled as she had nibbled practically all her life, like a scatter rat.

Lies passed over the rails under the wheels, the deceipts of decrepit old men whose navels moaned the requiems of death and whose bodies were pressed out from the center forming a moldy contagious disease on the inside linings of their putrid pain-stained raincoats and heavy grey flannel suits.

The colonies of toads that lived in strap fixings of the carriages became attracted by the entice of sweet steam spuming up in nicasmoke vape from Mr. Body's skull hollows. Soon Mr. Body's head was full of toads, the strapburrows empty except for necessary mating pairs to maintain the balance of life.

Pretty Bunch munched, and spat out her offal into a sack-like carryall; her hands drew sheets of glass over the pupils of her eyes, soon her head became closeted under prisms and prisms of windows; she got up and left at the next stop. The rustle of her long skirt of muscle fibers made church echoes along the platwalk. With a key she turned a tooth in her mouth and resumed her stance as a chocolate slot machine alongside a weigh-in and a rotting French dog on a wait bench.

Mr. Body had a compulsive, "the world of friends" maker parked next to him in Pretty Bunch's vacated seat.
"Blurt blurt blurt blurt blurt blurt," said friend. Mr. Body in all coolness lifted his sun poker, bringing it down slam on friend's head, friend leaked everywhere, amass of egg yoke. Mr. Body moved himself into the next carriage to avoid embarrassment.

❋

Key hived in a slum dwelling, or to give it the full eggs and trumpet, the Sir Arthur Lithuania Bling Busby slum estate, comprising amongst outside cess and indoor fungi, job lets, teatering breasts, clonky gutters, tap thru floors, stalagmites, dust plateaus, insectariums, suntop basements, and deathly emproy door knockers. Sir Ratha also amassed a chain of world surplus supermarkets. As the Squeaker Kids put it, marching in bottle dress and full threat –
>Clonk clonk clong, clink clink clink,
>ol' Artha slums one 'ell of a stink

Mr. Body's body was tied secure to a steep ramp which led to an estuary milked with the flow of silk-worm puke. Lady Jiver lifted her speech and proclaimed, "Poop, poop, poop, poop, and all who sail in her." With her right hand, Lady Jiver twisted an ear, releasing the ties that held Mr. Body HMS to the ramp, whilst the momentous swing of a lit cigarillo stubbed itself out on the soles of the good ship's feet. Mr. Body HMS tobogganed like a dead corpse into the ensuing tide.

Twelve old Navajo headless scalps adorned with war feathers pulled Mr. Body HMS to the open sea, just to the horizon, where the sun sea and sky met for sunset.

*

All wonky wainwilt from his morning stimble, Key opened a tin of day laxer easy chair, sat down, and munched a cushion filled with depth charged walter and cresp. Thru the laxroom window Key could see the Daily Catholic carry his church over a bed of coals. Mouse-peas grew as vines from the vestry doors leaving a trail of handwrit words in Latin matutinas, but the priest was a nagualist and practiced a secret cult found existing in Central America. The lips betrayed the hands, the head betrayed the robe, the face betrayed the ground.

Holly breezes, Key thought, Polly Poopylene is still at Bed, she's probably missed radio bandbox and Little Archie on the street passing by, from the airways of horny dog winged tonsils of the BBC. Key shiffled to his Poopy's empty mug at bedside, that vessel so oft used to break early morning mouth fungi. "Poopy, wake up, it's time for big business, the first fart, and a look at modern times."

Poopy opened one eye, saw it was the wrong one, closed it, and opened the other. After deciding that one eye is no match for two, she closed it, and proceeded to open one eye and then the other in perpetual flutter. She did likewise with her mouth. Key grabbed her by her fleshy shoulder-blade handles and gave her a shake, spat up her nostrils and removed a bad molar with a corkscrew. Poopy uttered a few blurbs from the side fillings in the sidings of her mouth.

Poopy slowly rolled up her eyelids, securing them fast with her lashes and said, "I was dropping I was in a buttapacking factree, and after becoming aware of how I happened, I was confronted by a man in a white frock and a list made to work by strings, he seemed quite casual but not in the least nonchalant, he seemed quite at ease, I felt relaxed, not the least upset when he spread butta all over my natured body." Poopy then shivered and lost a might of body weight. She drew in a breath and held it for some time. The whites of her eyeballs swung forth for a moment. Poopy regained her strength and went on, "he spread your muggers marmalade over the top, stood back, his lips watering with spit, then very slowly he opened his mouth, as it widened, the cavernous orifice grew bigger and bigger, I was just about to holla out, screaming 'Rude Bertha and spleening Arabs' when you came in and awakened me."

With that Poopy arose, and like the lame man, picked up her bed and walked. Poopy walked to an opposing wall, crashed into it full frontal, sank to the floor, arose refreshed, and slipped on her slipperies, followed by her fine leather waff's kit and judicial wig dyed randomly by headsweat and the pigeons in the trees.

❋

Mr. Body lay by moonlight in an open grave, spreading layer after layer of moontan lotion with old wreaths of plastic Anthirrhinums. Above the graveyard wall floated a weightless marble floor upon which large glass marbles rolled, each filled with a vocal gland. Mr. Body sang the words to tunes of current popularity and as he did so the marbles scattered, each collided with another, creating a harmonious choral background filler, in complete accord and accompaniment with Mr. Body's solos.

For a moment the graveyard transformed with the music into a playground, the tombstones into dancing children with heads of solar flares; the vaults changed into roundabouts of asteroid belts, the flower wreaths into diapalmac castles of sand.

❋

There was a knock on the door, which left it as quickly as it had struck it, but just out of tempo with Key's heart, so he was able to hear it. Key, seeing the door was still shut, and none the worse for the knocking, opened it.

The outside, all that was kept to the outer of the door, rushed into Key's head. "Hey Key, there's no toffee melting on your head."
"I had it removed, I'm not feeling too good," murmured Key. Rist pushed past Key to get inside, to relieve weight on the terrible burden brought to bear on the outside. Key, seeing the outside lightened, closed the door. And patted his head into his bowler helmet which he wore on secular occasions. Rist parked his bipedal in the center of Key's living room. "Hey Key, remember that lip trick you showed me. Well, forget it, watch this!!"

Rist let the banana of his flies go, and his Fruit-Of-The-Loom fell to the unrestraining forces of gravity. Staring down at his bounder with the utmost concentration and mental limbo, Rist implored, saying, "Kiss me, come on, kiss me!" Slowly Rist's Membro-Gladatori started to wax out, straight in front of him, like rhubarb being filmed over night with a time lapse camera.

When Rist's marauder reached four feet and a wee baby's lick, the heat from the fire in Key's grate wended the Holy Gobbler to the right, then homed back in an arc to the open corporation refuge truck of Rist's gaping mouth. Rist smucked an endearing smeck on the cup of his cobra. Key's eyes glonked clean out of his bonewaste, glued to the magic set before his humble person.

"Hello Poopy," said Rist. Key's head shot about to where Poopy was standing. Poopy, her eyes smarting, her knees quivering, must have been standing to attention by the door for quite some time. Rist repacked his things, like a grand silent Olympian, and Poopy ceased a salute which bore a great stain on the buttons of her battle tunic.

❉

"OK, Mr. Questor, put me in," said Mr. Body. Questor opened the door of landscaped freeze-meat storage unit. Mr. Body entered within, locking the door behind him. The icescape resembled the polar ice cap, one thousandth scale, miniature ice flows, pack ice, glaciers, peaks, and ridges, with thoroughbred fauna also to scale, miniature penguins, sea lions, sea birds, etc., moving in scurrying formation like particles of dust on a windswept pavement.

Mr. Body started cutting a hole with his ice pick into a sharply defined iced atoll. After chipping away ten centimeters, he found what he was looking for: a chrome plated handle. Mr. Body pulled against the handle using the entire weight of his body.

A crack emerged, then a split, and the whole icescape cut apart down its center. Mr. Body heaved again, raising both halves of the landscape, as one raises double trap doors in a false floor.

As Mr. Body lifted the landscape back, he locked the two halves with bolts into an upright position. Then, climbing down into the sky between, he comfortably stood in a relaxed position, all the time concentrating on the lifted underside of the two raised icedoors that resembled an expanse of smooth plate glass.

Soon kaleidoscopes of light danced on the surfaces, increasing by stages in brightness. The fauna of the icecap had been shifted through vibrating troughs linked to conveyors, then capsuled and stored for further use. This had been achieved with the use of the floor surrounding the ice doors, that is, between the doors and the landscaped walls.

Mr. Body gazed at his wrist watch, a magnetized miniature revolving replica of the earth, shaded in parts by darkness over certain meridians, to such precision one could conclude to its accuracy of within one second.

Slowly the sun rose beneath the soles of Mr. Body's feet, up through the sky shaft with Mr. Body perfectly balanced upon it. The monitors outside the freeze unit tracked the satellite with telescans. As Mr. Body's toadled head loomed near the ceiling surface, a technician pressed the corneas of his eyes with his fingers, causing the ceiling to splinter like the cracking of an addled eggshell. Soon the sun hung in its properly behaved place, kept at a constant temp with Mr. Body's toads and the acquired use of his sun poker.

✵

Oofer, the rude robot dog stray refuse eater, pulled at the winch chain clunked about its neck, a chain gripped at tether end with the fingles of little, flirty Mable from Squeaker Street. Oofer went clonk, clonk, quash, clonk, squash, clonk, squash, squash.

On this such occasion a shyknees man shovefell from the back exit of a shyknees restrunt, he was a waiter dressed in dishcloths. It seemed that his customers wouldn't eat him, so Oofer did. Squarsh, squarsh, clonk, wag, arsh, clonk-clonk-clonk wag squeash wag.

The above words do not compensate for Oofer's inability to talk. In fact, Oofer was capable of speech, perfect metal plated English; what was discordantly conveyed in buck-rattle was, "grapes sits good!"

Although the sky filled with green parrots, the only cloud strata to appear loomed over Trilly's Veterinary Acupuncture Clinic. Soon all was penitent and omnipotent.

Squoggy Little Mable of Squeaker Street had buttered plaits with hitched cords, cords that pulled the sun along. In turn, the sun melted the little toffee atop of Little Mable's head. This made her very happy. Her mind stumbled into thoughts of Trilly, Trilly of the Veterinary Acupuncture Clinic. You see, Trilly, concerned old Liberal of discontent, thought of away to stop dogs fouling the pavement, by the skillful use of acupuncture needles to the precise parts of the animals' anal rear. The idea worked for a time until pedestrians on the byways developed notions about pin cushions and their uses. Elderly ladies stuck hatpins in the poor creatures, hedgehogs fled to more secluded areas. But on the whole Trilly's experiment was a success, thought Little Mable, lovingly patting O.R.D.S.R.E. on the ass.

Little Mable of Squeaker Street and Oofer the clonky finally reached the half-demolished zoo of half-demolished jumble animauls. Lions and famous etcetera abounded like thro-away toast, and so did giraffes with felled necks, zebras with horizontal stripes. Of the lions only their bodies and tails remained, the lesser parts of a sportsman's trophy crumbling away.

Little Mable sat upon a lion to prevent it making rearable telephone calls to game park homelands. Oofer belched in bulk, and an elephant's trunk snacked and fell, making it very difficult for the midget brimston to take off in his tiny oster. A leopard's tail was went and fell, blocking up a main drain. When all was quite quease, Little Mable went ahead with her telling Oofer likable droop-inducing myths, chilblains stories in Cameo, like Harry Embro.

Harry Embro never ate; he was a flavor digestion freak. He'd cook himself a hot meal and sniff it 'till it was cold. Somehow he derived out of that all the nourishment he needed to sustain his life. He could heat up the same mess of vittles one hundred and twenty times before the digestible smells had diminished. But Harry had problems. After about twenty heatings of his favorite beef steak in grave, the after effects became dangerous. Strong potent poisonous and ruminatory vapors issued, killing all animal life in sight.

Harry was advised by his local practitioner to go and see Doctor America for an anal suppressor, a long metal tube-like hand gun silencer, deposited half embedded in the passage and taken out at night. Doctor America lived in the middle of a vast desert wherein V.D. Ladies Clubs loomed and multiplied everywhere for the enjoining of venereal ladies. There were fortune tellers who read skidmarks in jockey shorts. Doctor America found it a little difficult getting the silencer in, and by a freak of irony had to use a freeze compound of explosive ruminatory vapor, pharmaceutically encapsulated in a crush-proof capsule. This did the trick; Harry Embro's new anal suppressor was a huge success. By means of contract, he vowed to bequeath it to the nation after his death.

Soon little Oofer was asleep, whirled up about Squeaker Street Mable's feet, and there Oofer drooped 'till it was time to let the sun go. By then Oofer's body had deyeasted the refuse. As he lay adroop with sleep, his anal traps splewed out dinky handfuls of food pills, recycled tabs of roast beef and two veg, bled and buppy, chocolate bickies and all manner of savory salvos. Lobo of Squeaker Street myth of ages past, handled down from veneration to generation.

Never Take Candy From a Stranger

One bright Sunday morning, opening the big linen closet where she stored her sheets, Millicent discovered a pallid and somewhat shabby individual who seemed crammed into that piece of furniture which had come down to Millicent from her grandmother. She was beginning to feel astonished when she recognized what she was dealing with: this was a white-haired, gray-bearded, toga-robed and earth-shod gentleman of inestimable age whose beleaguered wings seemed to reflect a rather jaded mother-of-pearl appearance. My God!" she exclaimed, almost swallowing her fingers, when she realized the importance of her remark. The latter, without shaking off his uncomfortable mien, and with fingers locked to resemble an upturned crib, had taken a few steps into the room. He was rubbing his eyes so furiously one might think he suffered the irritating effects of global air pollution, or as if he had been up all night landscaping a piece of his estate; maybe the light of day simply dazzled him.

The old gentleman ruffled his feathers in a furtive way while from the corners of his lips he mumbled incomprehensible senilities, too jumbled to make any sense. "I must do something," Millicent said to herself, deciding not to bend her legs and place her nice clean knees on the grubby floor. She tried to start up a conversation. "Sir, - I can call you sir, can I?" she stuttered and at once felt ridiculous. "How on earth can you speak to him?" she mused, "if only I had my loose-fitting negligee on and a water jug from the old washstand on my shoulder, I might feel a little more apropos."

But she had succeeded all the same in catching the attention of the shoddy fellow who, seeming to discover Millicent's presence for the first time, rested his gentle contact-lensed eyes on her. "Just my luck," thought Millicent, "the very first time I enter 'the luxury four-bedroomed, large living area plus carport, chance-of-a-lifetime competition, I end up winning the booby prize." At the same time she noticed the visitor was afflicted with a slight strabismus that drew his eyes in and not only this, he seemed to dribble a lot.

"You wouldn't per chance haveth some malted milk? He asked straight out of the blue in a hesitant yet somewhat hoarse voice. And he began to stare at a copper crucifix hanging on the wall (another memento from Millicent's grandmother), and after a brief pause remarked: "Why do people meddle in my private affairs?"

Returning from the kitchen with a glass of malted milk, Millicent almost dropped it — there was our shoddy old fellow engraving his initials with one of grandmother's hatpins across the smooth surface on the back of the copper crucifix. The elderly gentleman looked embarrassed at first but then said, "It'll be worth quite a bit, as an antique," and drank down his glass of malted milk in one swipe, licking the drops on his beard with his long pink tongue. Millicent then tried to question him. "Do you by any chance know the sponsors of the Tasty Wheaties House-Of-Your-Dreams competition grand draw with cash prizes to be announced this week?"

Her interlocutor very quickly became uncomfortable, coughed, went red in the face, and, judging by how quickly he chose to ignore her question, she decided to let the matter rest. "I'm on vacation," he said, trying to cover up the fact that he had hiccups with the occasional use of his sleeve. "Oh!" countered Millicent, "aren't you taking the family?" "My son's (hic) goteth this new (hic) sauna project (hic) he's working on (hic) right now (hic.) He's building (hic) sauna baths in all the tourist (hic) resort areas; said he (hic) couldn't geteth away (hic.)"

Despite her highly developed sense of hospitality, Millicent ended up with the thought that she must not too easily make herself a slave to this unusual presence. Standing there, in the middle of the bedroom anyway, with his disheveled wings sticking out, he took up a lot of space. "Do you think I might be allowed to hang your wings up in the wardrobe? It's getting, well, it is rather claustrophobic in here," she said tactfully.

The old man explained that his wings were his own flesh and blood and that he could not lop them off just like that, but he apologized for the inconvenience and drew them in so that they over-crossed down the length of his spine. The accomplishment was not without incident for when he drew in his wings he knocked over a curio on the mantel. The object, a little plaster grotto containing a Saint Bernadette as high as a lead soldier and made in Japan, had been smashed to smithereens.

"Noteth to worry," he said, "I've just the (hic) thing," and thrusting his hand into the folds of his robe drew out a small nude clay model of himself when a youth and carefully placed it in the grotto adding, "Justeth the right (hic) size, too." "It's a good likeness," Millicent said, trying to hide her distress, then enquired: "What's that large birth mark, or is it a mole, between your legs?" "That (hic), my dear, ist thy special (hic) endowment," he replied with a mischievous gleam in his eye. Millicent looked a little perplexed, but then again she thought it not for her to fully understand the mysteries of the celestial orgasm.

Later Millicent tried to make him understand that if he wanted her to take him in, he could in return devote himself to light housework: she lived alone and her typist's pay did not allow her to avail herself of the services of a daily help. But he proved to be incredibly piggish in his habits. Twice Millicent caught him having a snack from the garbage can, and her neighbors complained more than once over his habit of sharing equally the "Nine Lives" they put out for their cats.

This was taking his "waste not, want not" policy a little too far, thought Millicent. What he managed to do best, though, was sweeping up. Nimbly prancing about on tiptoe and skimming the floor with his full set of plumage he was not without style and a certain old fashioned grace. From the point of view of harmony, the silky sound he produced this way together with the odd choreographed scenes from Swan Lake, were easily better than the throb of a vacuum cleaner.

Millicent was particularly fond of the ballet and would make a point of going to see all the major touring productions whenever they visited the nearby city.

As night was coming on, Millicent at first thought to give him the sheepskin bedside rug but she soon blamed herself for such an uncharitable thought. Then she considered her grandmother's old oak chest of drawers, an enormous piece of furniture, with drawer space enough to accommodate a whole army of seraphims, but after due consideration she decided that its value as an antique, an almost priceless heirloom, did not warrant its marketable consideration.

Anyway, she contemplated, there certainly could be no sin in sleeping beside the supreme ruler. After all, he was old enough to be her unfathomably great grandfather. So she invited him to share her bed. With a nod of consent, he unashamedly undressed. He did not seem to mind her watching him, despite her overanxious curiosity. She was disappointed, however, when she saw that beneath his winter-weight toga he sported a three-piece Nainsook, an outfit of coat, shirt and loose-fitting, knee-length pants made from a fine twill, designed for the country gentleman of the 1930s to enable him to potter about the garden during the summer months with a great deal of comfort.

Upon removing the above mentioned garments, he could be seen to sport what were commonly named at the turn of the century "The long and simple flannels of the poor," in other words, a balbriggan undershirt and a pair of stretchy seam drawers, complete with cotton-webbed inserts and ties around the ankles.

Millicent almost puked at the sight of his ecru-encompassment, but he soon had them off, revealing a small black rubber cup, about the size of a thimble, attached with a thin leather throng over his genital area. "Did you shave it off?" enquired Millicent, noting the absence of pubic hair. The old man put on a serious face and, his stuttering now gone, said, "See thy though maker, as finely plucked as a new born babe." For indeed not a follicle could be seen save the tousled hair of his face and scalp.

"What be beneath thy finger stool?" asked Millicent brazenly, an air of teasing in her voice and a tint of pinkness on her face. "Come child, sayeth I, come take thee a peek," he replied, taking her strongly by the hand. The old gentleman took the black rubber cup betwixt his thumb and forefinger and lifting it teasingly a fraction on one side proffered Millicent a quick view of that which lay housed beneath.

"Good God!" she exclaimed, not in the least aware of the import of her remark. "Is it a mole?" "It is indeed so!" bellowed the old man, yanking loose the throng and throwing the entire orthopedic truss to the ground. Millicent had had a few lovers, merited by the grace of her eighteen years, and if she lived alone, this was out of taste for peace and quiet rather than from natural coldness. But now, having divested herself of her clothing, she felt a strong, earthly lust. This she convinced herself was nothing more than an untamed, yet untapped, religious curiosity.

Millicent placed the moistened tip of her index finger on the tip of the mole and gently, soothingly, made tiny circular movements. Soon, like the nipple of her own breast, the mole tightened and grew erect. The like of this is best documented by the noted archaeologist Prof. Kisset, to which I refer:

> In regard to early Byzantine treasures, notably among some recently found frescos, a frieze believed to represent the supreme God, Giesoo, hermaphroditic deity of creativity, is, according to Prof. Julian Winthrop, the most important discovery since the tomb of Tutankhamun.
>
> This beautifully painted frieze, on the north wall of a temple in the ancient city of Jata just north of Jabal Al Akhdar in Northern Libya, depicts the naked man/woman God Giesoo (male down the left side and female down the right half of the body), holding in the left hand a small black rubber cup, about the size of a thimble, to which is attached a thin leather throng, whilst in the right hand the God clasps an earthenware pot of soil said to contain the seeds of germination.
>
> The figure stands upon a rug of bright vegetable pigments. The design of this clearly shows a number of puffy clouds from which a heavy shower of rain is

seen to fall into a knotted fringe of golden silk. The rug represents the symbol of androgynity. The genital area itself is covered by a small mole (male) over which is painted a small crimson circle (female.) The whole is best likened to the literary use of the common colon. Balanced horizontally on the crown of the head is a large Roman-like phallus, made of what appears to be a black, porous stone.

—From Prof. Archibald Kisset's *Penal Pollenies*, Vol. II (1869)

When Millicent beheld the fully fledged black, porous stone phallus, once a pitifully inactive mole, she did indeed bend her legs and place her nice clean knees on the grubby floor. "My, how warm the member seems. It would taste delicious," thought Millicent. "Alas," he said, "for thousands and thousands of years, forsooth, I have suffered in the arms of seraphims who hath not known the pleasures of love, for without the sensual parts of their bodies, they hath no need of it."

And so saying, he thrust his phallus into Millicent's earthy delight. Again and again and again they achieved the ultimate satisfaction, those blissful wellsprings that reside in a sweet space between earth and heaven itself. Tenderly enfolded in one another's arms, they momentarily dreamt, as even the stones themselves dream, of having retained as a bed sheet only the wings that, flapping gently, provided a little cool air on that warm spring night. Then, towards dawn, the fanning movement ceased – the supreme being was asleep, his head on Millicent's breast.

The following morning when Millicent, her hair still undone, moved close to her strange lover to wish him good morning, he rose to his feet and at that moment they both knew that he alone must for the sake of all mankind make the supreme sacrifice, the selfless act. Millicent, with despair in her soul, her heart heavy with sobs, gently pushed him in the direction of the big closet. He submitted willingly, docile, head down, in an attitude full of resignation, and Millicent closed the closet doors on him, turned the key and gave out a deep sigh.

Nine months later, on a night shrouded with fog, Millicent gave birth to an eight-pound baby girl with what was thought to be extremely rounded shoulders. Blonde and blue-eyed, the child gazed into the faces of three household neighbors: middle-aged women bearing rolls of paper kitchen towels and basins of hot water.

Since the day of departure, Millicent had never felt the need of opening the closet again.

Of the Pleasures Left in Life: The Back Patch

A spacious redwood deck
Over a mid-Med blue sky
With armadas of cloud-cover scampering left to right
For our cinematic enjoyment
A twin of black zero-gravity Walmart lounge chairs to support bottoms
When taking in sightings of pink and or scarlet trumpet vines
Clinging around parapets that support deck
Pines behind tomato-red or purple or lilac dusk
Plus heroic gray or green hummingbirds
Hovering in to observe sitters
Before zipping off to sup on bottlebrush bloom
And landing on the wind bending tops of the tallest evergreens
Over a dispersal of succulents and common fruit trees
Distressed by drought

Orthopedic Woman Blues
(A Dystopian Blues Song)

Performed to the song of B.B. King's
Did You Ever Love a Woman
With Honky Tonk Piano

1.
I've got an orthopedic woman
Wears a leg brace all the time
I've got an orthopedic woman, children
Wears a leg brace all the time
Every time she moves her eyeballs
I get jumpy all the time

2.
Oh, I never have to worry
When I come home late at night
Yes, I never have to worry, people
When I get home late at night
I just rip off all the Band-aids
See if everything's alright

Chorus:
She's got splits under her toe nails
And bandages over her head
Takes the stitching out of her entrails
Every time we go to bed

3.
Oh, I've got an orthopedic woman, people
And her wheelchair's looking good
I've got an orthopedic woman, oooh
And her wheelchair's looking good
Just climb into a stretcher
And do all the things we should

4.
Well, I took her to the clinic, people
Needed dressings changed down there
Well, I took her to the clinic, people
Needed dressings changed down there
When the nurses went for coffee, oooh
Had a ball in after-care

Chorus:
Oh, I never have to worry
When I come home from the job
Keep a washcloth at the ready
Just in case we need a swab

5.
I've got an orthopedic woman
Wears a leg-brace all the time
I've got an orthopedic woman, children
Wears a leg-brace all the time
Every time I go to squeeze her
We commit the perfect crime

(repeat last two lines)

Every time I go to squeeze her, oooh
We commit the perfect crime

✳

Performance piece written in Montreal, 1976-1977

Rhyming Pearls About Elderly Girls

There was an old lady from Wapping
Who leapt from a rocky outcropping
It was quite a feat
Landed on both of her feet
Without dropping an item of shopping

There was an old lady from Woking
Severely addicted to smoking
She chain-smoked all night
Set her two lungs alight
Then a fireman gave her a soaking

There was an old lady from Cleethorpes
Who's very much into all tree sports
By her toes she would hang
Like a chimp who stole jam
But her passion lay in male board shorts

There was an old lady from Tooting
A crackshot at parashoot shooting
She shot a chap down
In a hospital gown
Plus a catheter used for polluting

There was an old lady from Bath
Who shaved her wig for a laugh
Her ears stuck out
And her snout suffered drought
But her rissoles one can't do without

There was an old lady from Staines
Who dribbled on seats of airplanes
Her sputum was such
It burned up her crutch
And smelled like a wombat's remains

There was an old lady from Pancras
Whose hubby was often cantankerous
She bought him a swab
To stop up his gob
Now his complexion looks cancerous

There was an old lady from Penge
Upon her neighborhood she'd avenge
Pull up her weeds and toss them next door
Until her garden could grow no more
Then the Smiths undertook their revenge
Tossed them back with a few from their friends

There was an old lady from Clyde
Washed her body each day at high tide
Her skin was so smooth
She was trying to prove
One can age looking like a backside

There once was an old lady from Stoke
Who survived after multiple stroke
They cut her apart
To look at her heart
But the strength of her love was a joke

There was an old lady from Grimsby
Who invented a musical frisbee
When she gave it a spin
Music came from within
But the singing was downright grisly

There was an old lady from Tring
Who looked like a rose during Spring
But when Fall came around
All that anyone found
Was a sleepwalking scarecrow with string

There was an old lady from Socket
Who grew most of her vegs in her pocket
In her hats she grew pulses
With the aid of osmosis
But her grandkids suffered sclerosis

Post-Christmas Dystopia

On the thirteenth day of Christmas
My partner gave to me
A stale turkey sandwich just for free

On the fourteenth day of Christmas
My partner gave to me
Two sad and rootless fir trees
And a stale turkey sandwich just for free

On the fifteenth day of Christmas
My partner gave to me
Three cups of tepid black tea
Two sad and rootless fir trees
And a stale turkey sandwich just for free

On the sixteenth day of Christmas
My partner gave to me
Four scratched-up discs by Enya
Three cups of tepid black tea
Two sad and rootless fir trees
And a stale turkey sandwich just for free

On the seventeenth day of Christmas
My partner gave to me
Five blinking strings of lighting
Four scratched-up discs by Enya
Three cups of tepid black tea
Two sad and rootless fir trees
And a stale turkey sandwich just for free

On the eighteenth day of Christmas
My partner gave to me
Six kicked-in plastic reindeer
Five blinking strings of lighting

Four scratched-up discs by Enya
Three cups of tepid black tea
Two sad and rootless fir trees
And a stale turkey sandwich just for free

On the nineteenth day of Christmas
My partner gave to me
Seven soggy cardboard Santas
Six kicked-in plastic reindeer
Five blinking strings of lighting
Four scratched-up discs by Enya
Three cups of tepid black tea
Two sad and rootless fir trees
And a stale turkey sandwich just for free

On the last day of Christmas
The garbage hauler said to me
Eight stinking bags of food waste
Seven soggy cardboard Santas
Six kicked-in plastic reindeer
Five blinking strings of lighting
Four scratched-up discs by Enya
Three cups of tepid black tea
Two sad and rootless fir trees
And the hauler's turkey sandwich thrown at me

A thoroughly side-splitting interpretation of the thoroughly side-splitting final half of a tale of a thoroughly side-splitting horse called Skobelef by the thoroughly side-splitting Norwegian writer Johan Bojer – #14B

From *The Once Upon a Time Stories*

O nce upon a time lived a thoroughly hilarious horse with the ridiculously amusing name of Skobelef. For weeks, happy, busy little feet had been leaping with joyous tidings to all riotous corners of the jovial parish. Peter Ho Ho Lo had bought a merrily registered thoroughly hilarious stallion who was not simply a laughing horse but could act the part of a whole stable of laughing horses of differing temperament. Only one grinning man could have turned the comic trick alone, and that was the chortling Peter Ho Ho Lo himself.

For the most part, the laughing horse walked on his amusing front and rear left legs but then after a bit changed to the two amusing right ones. The mirthful sight of this sent peals of laughter through those amused enough to see it. He kept whinnying in giggles even in his happy sleep. He was so fierce in his laughter that he had already killed a number of beaming men who, having suffered too many stitches, could not stop laughing.

And what do you suppose the thoroughly hilarious horse was fed? It was neither oats, bran nor laughing gas. The ridiculously amusing Skobelef's funny fodder was nothing less than funny-bubbles — champagne of a jovial vintage at that. It was commonly tittered that Peter Ho Ho Lo and his sunny stead munched this hearty provender together out of the same equally elated punch bowl. They required stimulants, the two of them. How else would they be able to bathe the countryside thereabouts in endless heavens of mirth?

To return to that particularly smiling Sunday, we were standing at the Church of Mirth keeping a hearty lookout across the exuberant parish. Peter Ho Ho

Lo was skipping his way to the blissful house of worship, merrily driving none other than the thoroughly hilarious Skobelef himself. The long line of laughing vehicles came deliriously rolling in from the convulsively jolly valleys. The line picked up lighthearted reinforcements at every rejoicing crossroads until it was like a delightfully pleasant bridal procession.

That lively day we kept our playful eyes on the fun-loving horses and estimated the people in the gigs according to their rapturously dumb, driven cattle. A whole sparkling universe passed in comfortable review, brightly fat and laughingly lean, jovially jaded and playfully fiery, old jolly-bellied nags with long charming necks and prominently playful backbones and heads contentedly sagging with each springy step towards the grinning ground under the bright burden of unceasing intoxication: prosperous-looking zestful brutes that gave manifest proof of good, happy crops and cheerful chunky bank deposits.

Look at that debonair brood-mare—she has freely weaned many a cheery colt and therefore carries her snickering head high and surveys the snorting world with sparkling maternal eyes. Here and there you can pick out funny fjord ponies with raggedly rascally haunches, carelessly stamping against the grade and sweetly sweating with the weight of the howlingly heavy gig, some of them so laughingly small that they make you think of sniggering mice. There comes a delightfully big old bay with huge happy watery eyes and graciously quivering knees, looking about as if to ask why there is no Sunny Sabbath for the likes of him.

Don't miss the beaming physiognomies of those virtuous, censoriusly side-splitting fillies proclaiming the sneering vanity of vanities, and just behind them wildly amused young gallants neighing at the he-he world in general. Have a look at that tender-looking bay gelding. Why is his pleased belly all spattered with leering mud? He is from an amusing mountain farm; early this joyously awake morning he had to wade through happy heath and giggly marsh, across smiling brooks and uproarious rivers on the way to the pleasing parish below where his mirthful master could borrow a rippingly funny cart. He has another titteringly tough time coming before he gets back to his sappy home. Talk about long hilarious processions!

But what has become of Peter Ho Ho Lo? Where is the ridiculously amusing Skobelef? At last, there comes someone driving behind all the sniggering others. He is still far away beyond the laughingly jovial farmhouses. Never mind, he is gleefully gaining ground at a pretty smart leaping pace. Hundreds of sunny eyes are fixed in rapturous attention. The cheery church bells ring out. Most of the merry horses have been unhitched and are tied to the big chortling ash trees. There they stand with their ridiculous uproariously funny heads buried in happy bags of stitch-inducing hay, grinding and grinning at their merry dinners and gazing elatedly about.

All of a sudden they jerk their jolly heads up, and even the most funny-boned fillies make shift to arch their amusing necks as they stare sunny-eyed down the road. The exceedingly dotty Peter Ho Ho Lo on the back of the ridiculously amusing Skobelef comes trotting outrageously before the giggling gig, a broad black sniggering hulk, his fetlocks heartily dancing, his merry mane sweeping in blustery billows down his raggedly, rascally neck, his laughing eyes shooting elatedly charged fire, two red sunny prize ribbons waving at his heavenly ears. He raises his chipper head and sniffs the mirthful breeze, grinning monarch of all he beamingly surveys. Then he lifts up his tickly voice, splitting his sides laughing.

Believe me, there was a thoroughly uproarious peal that fetched the hyenas out of the happy wilds. In the gig sat Peter Ho Ho Lo, holding the hilarious reins relaxed, a very debonair comic not over thirty-five funny years of age, broad in the smiley shoulder, vigorously vaudeville, smiling out the lobes of his ears behind bushy, bright sideburns. It was certainly too bad that his sniggering wife, sitting soppy beside him, was so much amusingly older than him; her every feature was pinned up in a grin, her rosy red cheeks were pinned in a grin, her eyes were pinned in a grin, the corners of her mouth were pinned in a grin, her ridiculously amusing voice was pinned in a grin.

As for Peter Ho Ho Lo himself, he had a weakness for all pretty, funny things, even for laughing ladies that were not heartily his own. As the ridiculously amusing Skobelef neighed at his side splitting affinities, Peter Ho Ho Lo glanced gaily at good grinning friends of his own among the rascally crowd and smiled. The ridiculously amusing Skobelef came to a screeching stop but got a cut of the elated whip; he cheerfully reared and got another mirthful stroke. Then he rapturously bounded up the funny road toward the hilarious parsonage, the happy crowd in his grinning wake, us rosy boys flying ahead like giggly birds on the wing.

It was a dotty circus to watch Peter Ho Ho Lo maneuver the ridiculously amusing Skobelef out from the sniggering shafts of the gig and over toward the soppy stable door. Peter Ho Ho Lo for sure looked sweetly swell that day; the thoroughly silly horse must have lent him a new sunny side dignity. His uproarious gray suit was so well brushed and he wore a side-splittingly stiff hat just like the jovial teacher's. But every now and then his peppy polished boots flew up in the merry air. The delightfully amused crowd stared for all they were worth.

Too soon, the delightfully magic horse disappeared behind the cheerily chortling stable door; presently nothing and nobody could hold their convulsive feelings any longer. Everything, Peter, Skobelef, the parish, the stables, the crossroads, the procession, the steeds, the cattle, the onlookers, the sunshine, the mountain farm, gigs and carts, church bells, heath and marsh, large trees boys in the first person, the text and the author, laughed so hard that the ridiculously amusing end to this story could not be cheerfully completed.

A thoroughly miserable interpretation of the thoroughly miserable first half of a tale of a thoroughly miserable horse called Skobelef by the thoroughly miserable Norwegian writer Johan Bojer - #14A

From *The Once Upon a Time Stories*

O nce upon a time lived a miserable horse with the wretched name of Skobelef. This was in the bleak days when the intolerable church bells of a dreary Sunday morning sent out their miserable summons, not over tortured highways and afflicted farmsteads, but over a miserable parish waiting to be convulsively wakened into miserable life by the drearily sustained, solemn calling of those wretched brazen tongues. The miserable bells rang and rang again, their miserable message set down in two miserable verses by the wretched Johan Bojer and due to miserable content excluded here from this wretched text.

And so the tortured roads grew pitifully black with agonized people on their dreary way to despairing church, some miserably on foot, some wretched on horseback. Miserable old codgers wheezed past, withered stick in one hand, uncomfortable hat in the other, their dejected coats under their painful arms and their miserable gray homespun trousers tucked miserably into their thoroughly wretched boots shiny with slime.

The suffering women trundled miserably along carrying grimy shawls and grief-stricken hymn-books and scenting the stinking breeze with their thoroughly foul-smelling handkerchiefs. Out on the miserable lake, bordered by thoroughly depressing hills and equally dreadful farms, appeared ailing row-boats driven over the miserable water by sturdy equally miserable oarsmen. From across the morbidly dreary fjord swept the pathetic sailboats. Far up in the depressing mountains it seemed as if the wretched cattle even stopped grazing, and the decrepit boy who was watching them put the thoroughly dismal goat-horn to his thoroughly miserable lips and blew a horrible stout blast down towards the pitiful folks at home.

In those dreary times, Sunday was both a painful holy day and a depressingly awful holiday. Looking back after these many miserable years, I have a dreadfully vivid impression that all the wretched world was tortured sunshine and dank green forests on an unpleasant day like that. The despairing old church, brown with sad tar, standing amidst the ugly crowns of mighty miserable trees, seemed then to be more than just a dreary building; there was something distressingly supernatural about it, as it knew all the boring details there was to be known. Many hundreds of tortured years had passed over it. It had seen the foul-smelling dead when they were barely alive, when they went to miserable church like our wretched selves.

The thoroughly morbid surrounding graveyard was a dreary little village of rotten wooden crosses and depressing stone slabs, and the dull green grass grew wild between the revoltingly ugly leaning monuments. We knew well enough that the miserable sexton mowed it to feed his mangy cows, so that when we got a joyless drink of disheartening milk at his oppressive house we felt as if we were quaffing the very cheerless souls of the miserable departed, a kind of dismal angelic milk from which we drew grief-stricken transcendental virtues with every rueful draft.

We thoroughly miserable boys used to dolefully stand outside the depressingly ugly church and do as our dull elders did — size up the mournful people who arrived after us. We judged by tragic appearances, and they all begrudgingly knew it. The anguished cripple made himself look pathetically smaller than ever so as to hide in the miserable crowd; the lugubrious dandies ran the sorrowful gauntlet of both oppressively friendly and unfriendly eyes, and haplessly pretty women looked down and smiled apprehensively.

We miserable youngsters searched the humorless gathering throng for someone to dispiritedly admire, some gloomy heroic figure we should like to bitterly resemble when we ourselves one day should be wretchedly fully grown. There was a woebegone new teacher, for instance, stalking along in his crestfallen face seeming homespun with his tragic-looking coat buttoned light, with a sorry looking white necktie, downcast top hat, and bleak umbrella. He was at least one miserable step up from being a glum farmer. Not a pensive doubt about it, we too were going to attend the wretchedly normal school. So we hopelessly thought, at any rate, until a blighted butcher came up from the thoroughly desolate city, wearing a somber suit of unhappy blue duffel, a dejected looking white waistcoat with a hopeless gold watch-chain, cast down cuffs, a dazzlingly careworn white collar, and a lamentable straw hat. He was a perfectly sickening revelation. With such a forlorn exemplar before us it was worryingly easy to decide that we were to become thoroughly miserable butcher's apprentices as soon as we were dejectedly old enough.

Many were the crushed magnates that paraded through our heartsick daydreams. Still it was no ordinary thoroughly miserable emotion that we laid blighted eyes for the first time on a jaundiced city lawyer. His was a truly morose royal presence. Even his heavy spirited nose had its forlornly appropriate ornament, a pair of dismally old eyeglasses. Our sickening ambitions soared beyond all desolate bounds. Whatever our hopes of heartsick education might be, most of us were bent on carrying our miserable studies far enough to impair our discouraged vision and so to justify the use of the thoroughly dismal gold rimmed glasses. Then came the thoroughly miserable Skobelef after all this miserable preamble made worse and seemingly never ending by the fact that the narrative up to this point is totally and thoroughly one which induces the reader to slit his own miserable throat and go wait to die in a thoroughly putrid puddle of puppy pee.

Therefore we shall bother not with the mundane exploits of the thoroughly miserable horse Skobelef and so ends our text.

Anglican Graffiti – Limericks in Free Form
Part 2

Here are fifty-two rhymes
From the comfort seat lines
On the walls of the halls
And the stalls at the malls
From the coarse to the simply sublime

#104
Have you seen my stripper named Cassandra?
Fire-eating thrill at Alhambra
She lit up the harbor
In Spanish Granada
Then dropped off the scene in Uganda

#105
Are you fully acquainted with Norma?
Got her kicks when attaching transformers
She'd wire herself up
Current shot up her butt
And she'd sing like a tremolo mourner

#106
Have you heard of a gal named Molly?
Whose war-scene tattoos were a folly
Grenades burst in her pits
Torpedoes got on her wits
And the tanks on her back fired off volleys

#107
There was a woman named Maude
Who wed a dumb English lord
Soon it was said
That from out of her bed
Came two morons and one with no head

#108
I have a gal named Ellen
To whom I keep on tellin'
With eyes always rollin'
Over constant doom-scrollin'
Will end at the funny-farm yellin'

#110
There was a young babe named Clare
Who entered a torrid affair
She screwed on the carpet
But failed to mark it
You should see what she did on the stairs

#111
There once was a charmer named Mona
Who wooed all the lads in Verona
Her likeness was posted
And everyone toasted
The reputed Queen of Savona

#112
There was a young lass named Beryl
With a name like that, you think peril
But Beryl's no mess
No worries, no stress
And her pets? Not one of them feral

#113
There was a large gal named Nohr
Needed a push to get through a door
Her legs were so swollen and fat
Couldn't see where her two feet were at
Last Christmas she fell through the floor

#114
There was a young cutie named Clarissa
With love-making tattoos on her kisser
Suitors drawn by the traction
Of facial attraction
Signed their names on her neck for distraction

#115
There once was a gal called Lorraine
Whose cooking was more than a pain
It's not very nice
When you use too much spice
And your guts look like tripe in the drain

#116
There was a tough gal named Constance
Who'd never put up with much nonsense
If you trod on her toe
She'd deal you a blow
Then yank it right out of her conscience

#117
Have you heard of a female named Pru
Who cooked up a foul-smelling stew
She failed as a chef
No one knew she was deaf
And her dishes were chosen by few

#118
There was a poor maiden named Vera
No single young man would go near her
From her nipples hung bells
From her ears dangled shells
And her armpits were growing wisteria

#119
A feisty young filly named Phoebe
Was crackshot at firing a B-B
As the sad story goes
She was picking her nose
When shot by a misguided dweeby

#120
There once was a woman named Blanche
Whose hubby fell from a branch
His spirit returned in the night
Giving Blanche a horrible fright
Seeing spooks all over her ranch

#121
There once was a mermaid named Nellican
Who slept in the beak of a pelican
When the pelicans flocked
She feared being dropped
But she knew she would always be well again

#122
I know a gal called little Louise
Got all her husbands down on their knees
Once they were down she did what she pleased
From morning to night she teased and she teased

#123
There was a shrewd babe named Tina
To date her, you'd need a subpoena
Once into your pants
She'd grab your expanse
And issue a stiff misdemeanor

#124
There once was a hip chick named Hannah
Who sang and played boogie piana
She was cool on the jumps
Kept the beat in her pumps
And took you way down to Savannah

#125
A pretty young gal name of Fadwa
Came all the way here from Padua
She seemed quite plain
Even hated the train
Yet we failed, what a shame
To find rhyme with her name

#127
There once was a spunky Priscilla
Who rode on the back of Godzilla
She showed with no clothes
At many tent shows
But her high coitus act was the killer

#128
There's a trans-gender lady named Cleo
Whose sex changed over to Leo
She loved her new ploy
Plus being a boy
And often took trips down to Rio

#129
There once was a gal named Dale
Who ate up all her junk mail
Coupons, handbills and cards
Sample bottles, in shards
Beside party favors gone stale

#130
There once was a vixen named Dusty
Whose breath was so foul and musty
It killed off her acne
And warts on her back knee
That made her more brazen and lusty

#131
There once was a gal named Finella
Who confined herself to the cellar
But you should see her fella
Who dressed in bright yella
And looked like a slick Cinderella

#132
There once was a maid named Theresa
Who lived on a diet of pizza
She looked rather nice
Liked a thick extra slice
Of cheese and sardines as a greaser

#133
There was a tough lady named Corrie
Who worked like a mule in a quarry
Her head crushed the stones
As she sung like Tom Jones
Then a landslide became her last folly

#134
There once was a babe named Frosty
Whose medical bills were quite costly
She traded her gems
To most of her friends
Spent the rest of her life on the mends

#135
There was a young miss named Minnie
Whose voice was so sharp it was tinny
Her hair was so strong
She resembled King Kong
And her lobes hung so low they looked silly

#136
Have you heard of a lad called Lonnie
Whose favorite tune was Old Swanee
Enjoyed songs about drones
And wolves with the moans
And daredevil odes about folly

#137
Have you heard of dozy old Dottie?
Who dwelled in a dream-covered potty
Her possessions were few
Just a pan for spit stew
And her grated earthworms tasted grotty

#138
Have you heard of Megan the pagan
A skinny young vegan from Macon
She'd read all her bible
In languages tribal
But cussed on busses when idle

#139
There once was a guy named Lou
Whose balls were infected with flu
The vet who's a niece
Simply smeared Fancy Feast
And the cat nodded once since he knew

#141
There was a young man named Paul
Played a good round of bowls with his balls
They returned when he whistled his calls
And rolled over the green
Like nothing you've seen
Then bounced with delight, over walls

#142
Young Johnson was always a rake
Whose sex organs all were a fake
Made of sausage and hard boiled eggs
And nothing to show for the vegs
His wife was all the same way
Her sex organs, fish of the day

#143
There once was a writer named Sages
Who wrote Butt-Wiping Down Through The Ages
Sold millions – he was asked to write more
A paperback aimed at the poor
With a scatter of pull-out pages

#144
There was a poor chap named Martin
Whose balls disappeared 'cause of farting
They found many to thank
When the all-vegan crowd was departing

#145
There once was a poor sod named Rookie
An original short-order cookie
His best was a roast
Of dog's testes on toast
With topping of skin that looked gooky

#147
There once lived a girl named Greta
An all-round world-champ bed-wetter
Without mattress put in
She learned how to swim
Now she can sleep much better

#148
A gun-toting cowpoke named Cobb
Enjoyed looking lewd for the Mob
The girls lapped it up
Ate his undies for luck
In the hope he'd be fit for the job

#149
There once was a chap named Roberto
Who wrote The Divorcee's Concerto
He tried a sonata
About a regatta
But results turned out a no-starter

#150
There was a young fella named Banes
Whose girlfriend loved sniffing his Hanes
In a stupor one day
She was carried away
And they say she died from his stains

#151
There was a young lady called Mabel
People thought she lived in a stable
'Cause she'd fart every day at table
And all of the chairs, she'd disable

With a cork in her bunghole she's able
To target her mark without cable
From coast to coast spread the fable
That she rendered ten ranch-hands unstable

#152
There once was a gal named Heather
Whose eye-color changed with the weather
They were gold in the sun
And in winter looked fun
But in springtime her charms came together

#153
There was a young child named Holly
Who grew to look like her dolly
When the doll came of age
Doctors built her a cage
Away from an amorous golly

#154
There once was a girl named Contessa
Who kept her defense in her dresser
In the top drawer her blade
Beneath silk ropes hand-made
In the bottom her breathing suppressor

#155
There once was a woman named Tasha
Whose frame was as thin as a rasher
She tried all her life
To be a good wife
But eloped with a dwarf haberdasher

#156
There once was a girl called Vanessa
The ways of the world would obsess her
But nothing on earth could repress her
Just those without love could depress her
And with them she served as confessor

#157

A wonderful gal named Coretta
Had posted her last email letter
In it she told she felt better
A breathless moment had met her
After death had stopped off to get her

#158

There once was a girl named Matilda
Who married a bird-nest builder
He'd work all the day
When the birds were at play
Our Mattie spent time with a gilder

#159

Do you know an old lady called Ivy
Who sang T.B. Blues like Miss Spivey
She could belt out the blues
Some folks lost both their shoes
You'd think it some kind of connivery

Opal's Book of Maladjusted Proverbs
(Anglo-American Edition)
Part 2

1. He that hath his flies undone cannot sprawl beneath the sun

2. She who hath plenty of sex will start on the animals next

3. He that marries a widow may often find naught on his pillow

4. He who runs like a flash makes the fastest cash

5. He who feeds all gets nothing at all

6. Some light candles and sing on a Sunday
   Then raise glasses in pubs on a Monday

7. She who talks to herself rarely takes dictation

8. He who thinks too much rarely removes false teeth

9. He who picks his nose rarely clips his nails

10. He who travels far puts mileage on his car

11. He that will eat the colonel must leave some for his troops

12. He who wants to enter paradise must find a good hacker

13. He that wipes the child's nose leaves deposits on his clothes

14. He who woos the lady's maid must be quick and always paid

15. He that must have good luck with the parson's wife
    Must drop much on the collection plate

16. She who needs to sin must wear her undies thin

17.   He who rides on a tiger may never enjoy his stripes

18.   He who swells in prosperity may shrivel in abject poverty

19.   Health and wealth create stealth

20.   His duckets burn holes in his buttocks

21.   History depletes itself

22.   Honest men marry late, older men vegetate

23.   Honesty is the best policy if the wife pays the insurance

24.   Honor and profit sit well in one pocket

25.   Hope for the best and pray for the rest

26.   Hunger finds no fault with the crockery

27.   I cannot be your friend and smell your laundry, too

28.   I gave the mouse a home and now it wants a phone

29.   I love thee like pudding, all crumbly & hot
      With whipped cream & raisins, dropped on the top

30.   I taught you how to swim, now you'd rather I fall in

31.   I was not born yesterday — I spent nine months in custody

32.   I will keep no more cats 'till their colors all match

33.   If the bed tells what it knows, the sound would deafen angry crows

34.   If the mountain won't come to Mahomet,
      He should shout with a rage at the summit

35.   If you deal in the street, think of all those dirty feet

36.   If you kiss the mistress, never diss the maid

37.   If you pay not a servant his wages
        He'll kill you with poison in stages

38.   Sharing our wealth can save everyone's health

39.   In a thousand pounds of law, not a penny goes out to the poor

40.   In one ear and out his mother's

41.   On a hilltop you will find
        A home to house the deaf and blind

42.   It's a poor dog that's not worth the whistling
        A sickly child that's not worth the christening
        A poor heart that never rejoices
        The grocery shelf with limited choices

43.   It's a gammy knee that's not very sound
        A lousy steak no better than ground

44.   It's a sad burden to haul a dead man's undies
        It's a bad omen to spit in church on Sundays

45.   It's a sad house where the mice round up the cats

46.   It's a sin to steal a sin; It's a sin to give it back

47.   It's better to marry a dumb blonde than a chatty brunette

48.   It's easier to raise the devil than bury the dead

49.   It's easier to play basketball up-slope than to play golf downhill

50.   It's better to rob an orchard when you're close to starving to death

51.   It's hard to be wretched but worse when expected

52.   It's good to have friends to burn candles both ends
        Than kill your cousins and torture your friends

53.   It's hard to be spliced, and not cuss at the wife
        Or get sloshed with whisky or gin

It's not hard to quit sin, and to keep her real thin
But the problem is changing your life

55. It's easier to pretend poverty than to bear it
When money comes in, you don't need to share it

56. It never rains until it soaks
And then it's time to take to boats

57. Knowledge means college
And detention means porridge
Which would you choose to acknowledge

58. Lightly come, lightly go
With nothing very much to show

59. The slain in Spain
Are buried with a crane
This dumb refrain
Is driving me insane

60. Make hay while the butt shines

61. Many a true word he often confessed
Once and for all, get it off of his chest
He blurted it out, the way he knew best
Wearing no trousers and pink spotted vest

62. March winds and May sun
Make clothes white and maids undone

63. Marriage is a lottery
That breaks like garden pottery

64. Waste not, want not
Give it to the have not

Species Pieces
(Unpublished Extracts)

#3 – The Common Seal (Phoca Vitulina)

Few animals have a finer sense of hearing than The Common Seal. Musical sounds appear to afford the seal great delight. Mr. Laing during his voyage from Spitsbergen often sat on deck playing his violin. This would generally draw around the vessel an audience of numerous seals who would continue in the wake of the ship and follow it as far as the English Coast.

#9 – The More-Pork Bird (P. Cuvieri)

A native of Australia, this fine bird derived its name from its cry of "More Pork, More Pork," loudly and distinctly uttered in rapid succession through the glades of the forests. For this costermongering remark, the bird was considered an ill omen by the first colonists.

#15 – The Jackal (Canis Aureus)

The shriek of the jackal terrifies the tenants of the night, breaks the stillness of the darkened hours with awful dissonance that rings among the ruins of ancient cities like the wails of legions of spirits over departed glories of other days.

#17 – The Cow (Taurus)

Upon the rolling slopes of Switzerland cows are seen to wear bells about their necks. If a single cow is seen to wander from the keeper's sight, the bell is removed. This never fails to reduce her to order, for she firmly believes that the sweetest grass responds to her peals and sings of its juices.

#19 – The Globe Fish (T. Pennantii)

A European species of plectognatha. It puffs its belly up and, overbalancing in the water, floats about on its keel displaying the barbs of its globe that resemble a floating mine, each sharp spine infused with electrical properties, driving away its enemy. War ships, mistaking them for explosives, cut a distance around them.

In the throes of death, The Globe Fish drifts toward the shore where it dies and becomes as hard as a gourd. Now a new life is thus begun for they are taken up by children who play sport with them.

#20 – The Dog (Canis Familiaris)

The dog is said to be descendant not from any single original wild stock but born of many and varied animals. The past is full of tales of dog-babes, dog-men and dog-women living perhaps wretched lives in dense forests and shambled parts of cities. Is there any truth in this?

The dog and the wolf breed readily, and their progeny are fertile. But the obliquity of the eye of a wolf differs from that of a dog. The wolf will rarely raise his gaze from looking down upon the ground unlike the dog who casts its eyes in a forward direction, a constant habit that for many successive generations is due to looking at its master and obeying the sounds of his voice.

#21 – The Hair Worm (Gordiacea)

This parasite of the insect world is at once distinguishable by the great length of its body that bears a resemblance to a horse hair, so close indeed in spirit and body that their ascribed origin is said to be the result of horse hair set in water to propagate. When exposed to great heat they dry up like a speck of dust and appear as dead as the ash in a burial jar, but rain will again raise them up for they live once more with the thirst of a vampire.

#2 – The John Doree (Zeus Fish)

This celebrated delicacy along European coasts is said to bear the prints of St. Peter's fingers for a golden spot marks the sides of its body where the impression of two gold coins were implanted in its scales to light its way to paradise.

This mark of honor is also associated with an old legend concerning St. Christopher who, when wading through the arms of the sea and bearing upon his back the sky-child, caught a Doree and left these impressions on its sides for fishermen to see and marvel at.

#25 – The Armadillo (Dasypus)

The sustenance of Armadillos consists principally of grounded fruits, earth roots and worms, but they do not reject the body-curds of half putrid flesh for they dig deeply into the graves of those bedded without enclosures of brickwork. On this carrion they grow swollen and corpulent and their flesh becomes of a tasteful excellence, esteemed as a great delicacy by the native peoples of the plains and savannahs of South America.

#26 – The Spotted Hyena (Hyena Crocuta)

The animal shows a preference for human flesh. It is found in great numbers around Mamboland in Southern Africa. It enters the beehive-like dwellings of the Mambookies in the pitch of night, passing by the tethered cattle. Being not afraid of fire, it creeps by the sleeping adults where they lie for protection. It proceeds to where the children are sleeping and takes them from under the mother's kaross in so gentle and cautious a manner that the cry of the innocent child is only heard when the monster closes its jaws.

#30 – The Dugong or Small Indian Whale (Halicore Dugong)

The Dugong is all heart. In fact, the Dugong has two hearts, and when a Dugong falls in love – the Dugong falls very much in love – four hearts in love in two bodies. The male and female parents are inseparably devoted and this affection spills over onto their offspring, for they have two hearts, too. So devoted, so much in love is the Dugong that when one of a couple is killed by harpoon, the other surrenders without the least struggle.

#31 – "The Bell Bird" (Arapunga Alba)

The "Bell Bird" is found in the lush forests of Guinea. It measures but a foot in length and is dressed in the purest white, like the robes of a noble priest. Its voice resembles the deep tolling of a bell and can be heard at a distance of three miles during the heat of the day, as if calling all fruit crows, piper birds and true-chatterers to spiritual reunion when most other feathered inhabitants of the rain forests are hushed in the shades of silence.

#43 – The Robber-Crab (Pagurus Latro)

Thief of the Pacific, native of beautiful Amboyng and neighboring islands, this crusty naval vessel of immense proportion comes forth out of the fissures of rock at night when the shore's breath of winds tinder the stars for it to see its path to the cocoanut grove. There it ascends the pandanus odoratissimus palms and with its tweezered limbs splits the cocoa-shells to sup upon the flesh. Then odd sounds are heard, like the snapping of fingers in a fine French restaurant.

#44 – The Kangaroo (Macropus Major)

The gestation is the passing of 39 days. The appearance of the young one 12 hours after birth is thus described:

It resembles an earthworm by color and is semi-transparent of its integument, adhered quite firmly to the point of its mother's nipple. Like a sleeping child it breathes strongly but slowly and moves its forelegs in the spaces of its soft rest. The body is bent upon the abdomen in a coil of warmth, its short tail tucked between the hind legs that are two-thirds the length of the forelegs. The three divisions of the toes are now distinct.

The whole length, when stretched out, from the nose to the tip of the tail, is but little more than an inch.

If male, and into maturity, the Kangaroo can weigh as much as 220 pounds. It can swim and jump a distance of 15 feet. When attacked by a dog, it will snap it up in its forearms and, clasping it tightly, make away with it and finding a nearby water-hole, keep it beneath the surface until it is drowned.

#46 – The Processionary Caterpillars (Cnethocampa Processionea)

The soldiers of Southern Europe where their armies can be seen in sturdy oak fortresses, multitudes of foot-soldiers that gather into Roman legions, a party spirit driving them along the songs of the branches, left right, left right, the leader at the head, the brave pioneer, laying down paths of silk for standard bearers to follow, routes of instinct along which a single file passes at first, followed by platoons two abreast, and behind these platoons, three abreast, then four, five and six abreast, winding down to the roots of the tree like the thread of a wooden screw being worked into the crust of the earth.

#49 – "The Rose Leaf Cutter" (Megachile Centuncularis)

This insect is the tomb mason of the earth, the master builder, the wise philosopher whose art is architecture, whose scientific principles are based upon the laws of unconscious geometry.

The Megachile bores a burrow in the earth and constructs a series of thimble-cells where she will pickle her young in spheres of glass. First she will cling to the lower edge of a rose leaf, her limbs clasping tightly. Then, cutting neatly a circular piece with her mandibles, she will pass this to her legs so as not to impede the progress of the fretwork. As soon a she has cut so far that her weight might tear off the piece, she poises herself on the balance of her wings, completes the severation and flies homeward to her gallery. During the flight she holds the circular portions of the leaves in a bent position, perpendicular to her body.

Upon arrival at the tomb, without glue or paste, trusting only the elasticity of the leaves (acquired in drying) to retain their position, she works her leaf, its center opposite the join of the two preceding ones. Each apartment is composed of 10 or 12 of these tile-like pieces so artfully retained one would not credit the makers of fine cigars the weaving-work of it. In the apartment thus composed, no better rounded than if she were to make use of a compass, she deposits a fluid of honey and pollen, gathered chiefly at the thistle, and colored like the fire of a rose.

Upon this is deposited the eye of an egg, oversealed with the lid of a leaf, forming a circle as true as that inscribed by Copernicus. To this, more apartments are added until the gallery is filled with the incubators of her heirs, the landships and thimbleworks of repetition whose ancestral ruins might well have underscored the continents with a lacework of pearls.

#50 – The Hoonuman Monkey (Semnopithecus Entellus)

In India, at a place called Dhuboy, a man may often wish to revenge himself on his neighbor for any insult or injury, and by this singular means he takes the opportunity:

Just before the periodical rains (about the middle of June) set in, and when the tiles have been adjusted to meet the season, he repairs to his neighbor's roof and scatters over it a carpet of rice or other grain. This is soon discovered by the Hoonuman who not only devour it but pull up all the tiles in search of what has fallen through the crevices.

At this critical juncture the rain commences, coming down in solid walls of glass. Under cover and not wanting to go outside, no single man can be found to re-set the tiles. The house heaves apart like a sinking ship, the furniture washes away into the forest, and the store of grains, generally formed of unbaked earth, drifts away like insects on the surface of a lake.

#58 – "The Blind Fish" (Amblyopsis Speloeus)

Once in a small lake within the great Mammoth Cave of Kentucky, the blind fish swam, turning in circles of eddying currents, spinning in waters through which its generations down through the centuries had sounded the boundaries, its eyes walled in with a lid of opaque skin, its anus situated at its throat, in front of its extra-sensory fins, for it is thought that the trails of its waste blazed a path to its destiny.

#80 – The Electric Centipede (Geophilus Electricus)

During English summer nights one may see lawns of glistening threads, tortuously blown by the winds, tides of illumination, their rings aglow, undulating as if smelting the green into copper plate.

#84 – The Ariel Gazelle (Antelope Arabica)

The huntsman advances as near as possible to the herd. The dogs are then slipped and the falcon thrown off. The individual animal that the dogs have singled out is attacked by the falcon that is trained to strike at her eyes so as to check her speed and thereby enable the dogs to reach her.

The Gazelle's eyes are peculiarly large, dark and lustrous and have supplied a simile to Oriental poets and creators. Indeed, to say of a woman "She has the eyes of a gazelle" is to them a most flattering commendation.

I would suggest to women who are thus flattered that it may be in order for them to acquire and train falcons so that they will prey upon such Oriental flatterers, in view of how they are wont to destroying such animals.

A Most Unlikely Story

have just written to the editor of the *Scientific American* to tell him that I have no option but to cancel my subscription. My reason for such an extreme action? Nothing less than the publication in his serious monthly periodical of a story so ludicrous that I myself would hesitate to put my good name to it. Yet they have had the nerve to print it as coldly as if it were an everyday event.

Well, when I buy the *Scientific American*, I expect to get something serous to read for my money. You do, too, don't you? Of course you do. But when serious people like the staff of the *Scientific American* decide to let their hair down, they don't do it by halves. And this time they have gone too far. Anyway, judge for yourselves. Here is the offending report, more or less word for word:

The Nobel Prize-winning Swedish naturalist Bent Gaslüngen of Uppsala, a Darwinian scientist, recently decided to follow a living organism through all the stages of evolution. Accordingly, he bought a smorgasbord sandwich that had been caught alive in the kitchen of a famous downtown Stockholm restaurant and put it under a glass pyramid that he himself had constructed in his laboratory using a kit from Psycho-zap, California. He sprinkled fresh olive oil on it every day, but always in a slightly smaller quantity.

As might be expected, this seemed to disturb the tomato, cucumber, ham and cheese on buttered rye to begin with. He re-adjusted the light and shade to a satisfactory incubated environment and began bit by bit to get used to a solitarily confined existence, thriving partly in air and partly in olive oil. So Prof. Gaslüngen took the experiment a stage further. He removed the glass pyramid. This naturally caused the smorgasbord sandwich to behave in an unusual way. As it became adjusted to its new surroundings, it began to disintegrate. First it seemed as though an invisible human gullet was masticating its substance. Huge bites seemed to break away from the whole and were chewed over by the ghost of two rows of powerful molars. The smorgasbord sandwich in its next stage of evolution was being devoured, or was in its own way eating itself.

Soon, a chewed mass of sandwich lay in an undigested heap. For the next part of the experiment, Prof. Gaslüngen replaced the chewed smorgasbord sandwich under the glass pyramid. Again, strange things began to happen. A curvature of intestinal skin started to form, wrapping entirely the chewed sandwich in the pylorus, fundus and antrum of the common Scandinavian human stomach. The cardiac orifice and lesser curvature were perfect.

Prof. Gaslüngen once again removed the glass pyramid and found that the digesting smorgasbord sandwich encased in its own "stomach" could thrive quite happily in an open environment. He squeezed it with his hands here and there and felt a certain sensuality akin to the sponge. Then he took it out with him for walks, or rather, for sport — he found it most suited for Rugby football – and kicked the hell out of it. No harm came of this as the "stomach" seemed to enjoy being kicked around.

Impatient to complete the final stages of the experiment, Prof. Gaslüngen once again put the digesting stomach under glass where, as the days and nights passed, it seemed to decompose, or better still, re-compose decomposed. A week later, Prof. Gaslüngen found he had created the perfect foul-smelling piece of excrement; here then was the final stage in the evolution of the smorgasbord sandwich.

But, sad to say, Prof. Gaslüngen found he could not remove the pyramid glass – a kind of bacteriological force field was holding it in place. The lump was becoming more evil-smelling every day. Something had to be done as it did not seem to dry out but somehow thrived instead in a fresh state.

He tried smashing the glass but nothing seemed to have any effect on it. "Alchemy was indeed at work here," Prof. Gaslüngen stated as the smell disappeared and the excrement gradually transmuted itself into gold. The perfect turd of gold.

Prof. Gaslüngen now found himself able to remove the glass pyramid and take the golden turd in his hand. Alchemist gold. "It was magnificent," he was reported as saying.

However, the stool of gold was swallowed by its natural predator, a ham, cheese and pickle sandwich some weeks later.

The 23rd Psalm
(Impounded Version)

My dog's a golden shepherd
He knows no end to want
He taketh me to sit down in green parklets
He leadeth me to cans and tap water
He exploits my soul
And drags me down the paths of playfulness
For his and for my sake
Yeah though he tugs me down the aisles
Through the shadows of bags full of dog-food
I shalt fear no mugging
For Thou art with me
Thy teeth & claws shall comfort me
Thou will rip up tablecloths before me
In the presence of outed in-laws
Over whom you anoint scolding tea
From cups Thou spilleth over
Surely the law and pet owners shall chase me
All the days of my strife
That I shalt dwell in the house with full-board
Forever

The James Boys

Extract from an unpublished book-length manuscript about Jesse and Frank James

The Battle of Centralia, Missouri, 1864:

Bill Anderson, a man with a reputation for being the meanest brigand in Missouri, gradually gained power over many of Quantrell's men. Anderson was soon honored as the bearer of the black banner. Quantrell, refusing to follow Anderson's leadership, retired to Howard County. Anderson rallied his guerillas immediately for a raid on the northeastern portion of Boone County, and on September 27th, 1864 rode at the head of his men into Missouri's Centralia, seething for revenge against the Federals.

Bringle, the scalper, rode with him, as did Todd, Poole, Arch Clements, the Hills and James Brothers. The rest of the savage gang followed in the rear, 150 in all, eager and determined to butcher anyone who stood in their way.

Centralia village straddled the St. Louis, Kansas City and Northern Railroad, ordinarily a quiet and peace-loving place, but as soon as Anderson and his men drew rein in the streets, citizens shuttered their windows, took their children off the streets and hid themselves. The fear the guerillas inspired gave them easy possession of the village, and taking this to full advantage, they plundered and pillaged every home.

Around the time their ravages were concluded, a train of cars, loaded with soldiers and civilians, pulled into the depot, 28 soldiers in all and for the most part unarmed. What could 28 soldiers do against 150 desperate guerillas, armed to the teeth? Nothing, save to throw themselves at the mercy of the savage band.

Anderson lined them all up along the railroad track, then, separating soldier from civilian, picked four blue-bloused recruits and slaughtered them like so many sheep. But the sun scarcely had time to dry the blood on the bodies of the fallen Federals when 100 Iowa cavalrymen rode into Centralia, and the bloodstained tragedy continued. The cavalry fought with great courage, but many lives were lost before Major Johnson rallied his decimated forces and charged straight through guerilla ranks.

Anderson's men now numbered 200, and when George Todd ordered them to surround the troops and close in, they slaughtered the cavalry almost to the last man. Mercy held no sway in guerilla law. Jesse spurred his horse straight for Major Johnson; one bullet tumbled the major from his saddle. It was all over. Few got away to tell of the terrible massacre.

Frank James cut down eight men that day. September 27th, 1864 will for ever hold a bloody place in Missouri records of the Civil War.

– Cambridge, MA, 1980

The Kindly Physician

What happens when you fall ill? You call your neighborhood physician and if, after repeated attempts, he fails to get you to crawl on your belly through six feet of snow and howling winds in a temperature of minus 30 Celsius, he may decide to make one of his almost extinct house-calls to your sickbed. So rare were these house-calls that neighbors stand on corners to take pictures, press and T.V. camera crews hasten to the spot so that when your physician finally arrives at your apartment, chances are your local priest will have finished the final prayer and is wrapping up his bible.

Let us assume hospitalization is out of the question. There is a line-up for vacated beds stretching from now until the time when the beds in question fall apart with rust, old age or disinfectant.

You succeed in getting your physician to call on you, and for this, like all star appearances, you offer to pay him as one might God's own healer for this is the going rate. He feels you all over like a rare dob of prehistoric putty, taps your chest with excruciatingly cold fingers and allows himself to ask you a few questions, all with his mind meanwhile far away in a place where a great multitude of sick patients are pushing and shoving to touch or grab hold of the hem of his garment.

He then writes out the customary prescription in the language of the Rosicrucian or disciples of Paracelsus and says "I'll tie a rope to your bed leading down the stairs and out along the sidewalk to my surgery so that the next time you need to see me you need only hang on and haul yourself along at your own speed." So, like greased lightning, he passes out the door, makes a pass at your wife, until it comes to pass one day that you quietly pass away, at which point scores and scores of leaflets from funeral homes flood your mailbox and traveling salesmen wearing black suits and carrying miniature models of wooden boxes call every other minute at your door. After all, the lucky winner has to give his cut to the physician who in turn is reminded of those bulky lump sums of cash he may acquire if he helps to recommend said services should occasion permit.

If you do manage to avoid serious illness (which is not too difficult) and submit to his treatment (which is virtually impossible), the good physician will still be rubbing his hands and caressing his pocketbook with glee because every visit means a bag of gold from you and a bumper commission from your pharmacist. Very soon it all snowballs into a new yacht and a villa in the sun for him to visit on weekends.

The only thing that makes a physician sad is when you recover immediately. If there is capital left in your bank account, he will swiftly turn to emergency tactics; with the right medicines, he can quickly make your flesh a nice, unhealthy green again.

One day when I woke up in a cold sweat, or maybe a hot sweat (I can never tell the difference when in the presence of a hot water bottle), I realized I had caught a dose of "*the nasties.*" I phoned my physician and, as he had planned to be in my area, he kindly condescended to pay me a call.

During the ensuing weeks he prescribed various medicines which brought to light various symptoms which prompted more medicines which indicated more symptoms which instigated more medicines which brought to bear more medicines which identified more symptoms which indicated more medicines until the inside of my stomach resembled a bubbling vat in a Salvation Army soup kitchen.

Within a few weeks I was a veritable skeleton, emitting smoke through my ears and the foulest type of living waste material through my bowels. By then I had hocked all my worldly possessions to pay for the treatments and found myself without sheets, blankets, bed and mattress, huddled in the corner of my bedroom in an apartment stripped of all furnishings, but completely jammed from floor to ceiling with small bottles, packets of pills, boxes of ointments and rolls of bandage.

Then one morning when I was feeling absolutely wretched, having slept on a bed of stone-cold sleeping pills, my physician called to examine me, this time rather more thoroughly than usual.

Quite happy in this apartment, are we?" he said.
"Yes, of course," I replied.
"How much rent do you pay?" he asked.
"$250 a month," I said.
"Landlord OK?"
"No complaints," I said.
"Good, well then, I ..."

"What are all these questions leading up to, doctor?" I said somewhat puzzled.
"Well, to be quite frank," he said, "I've been looking for a flat like this for quite some time," he said checking the walls for bugs.
"Yes, but I have no intention of moving out."
"Perhaps not, but you may have to in the near future."
"Move? Move Out? But why?"
"Ah, well …"
Suddenly I caught the drift.
This savior of the ailing spirit thought that I would soon pop off, go to bye-byes so to speak, and he was trying to tell me so in no uncertain terms. I can hardly tell you what effect this curt revelation had on me:

A terrible sort of artificial malaria to begin with, then a mock epileptic fit followed by a loud scream which toppled a pyramid of tiny bottled time-capsule pills, and broken glass scattered everywhere. This was followed by a sort of cross-eyed, blind rage. "Is this the way you treat a sick man!??" I screamed, inching my way up the wall in an effort to stand on my feet. "Is this the way to treat a customer, and a good customer at that?" I raved, tottering sideways and hurling family-size bottles of Formula 44 at the rubber cups of his stethoscope.

"So you'd like my flat, would you, my friend?"
Let me just pause a moment to say that there is nothing quite like a tremendous rage to cure the evils of sickness for I found my lost strength immediately, and by taking my man of medicine by the seat of his pants, I quite easily threw him down the stairs.

By putting up large, bright signs in my window I managed to sell all the medicines at "one time only" discount prices and from the profit made was able to refurnish my apartment with enough cash left over to buy the building from the landlord and convert all the other rooms into tasteful apartments for my newly acquired private hospital.

The Man Without Features

Poor Uncle Bill awoke one recent morning and felt like a peeled orange. He gazed wearily into his bathroom mirror and discovered that most of his facial features had gone to the devil – eyebrows, eyeballs, Roman nose, earflaps and false teeth. He could not believe this. His celebrated life had bested the Boy Scouts with all hard-earned achievement patches. Only the week before he had the sensation of losing his nipples. Around midnight last Wednesday, the twin peaks of his nipples fell off, rolled over the bedroom floor, then slid between the cracks of the floorboards. Poof! Gone! Total rejection! But that was different. Within minutes a fresh, all purple pair of nipple-work grew over where the former had been in what seemed like a split second.

Uncle Bill's eye-sockets instantly lit up like spare battery replacements. The ensuing light indicated to him that only his nostril cavities, mouth and inner ear canals seemed back in place. Never ever a religious person, Uncle Bill would not think to call upon a deity or a devil. He simply hollered with alarm. Cats leapt up, dogs cowered and children everywhere fell out of bed. The thunder of the fall seemed like impending doom had arrived, all because of a quiet, like a lamb wearing two wool coats.

Uncle Bill's face evoked never ending deserts with twin rabbit holes gathered about. They took on the appearance of earlobes and nostrils. Uncle Bill never once looked for a second life up to now. He was content with his first one. It was not long ago Uncle Bill had imagined that his tongue had evolved into a razor-edged trowel-blade that although firmly attached rattled like crazy in his mouth. Was this an omen? A warning of something evil to come? Uncle Bill then felt a strange release. In tandem he felt the opposite experience, the grasping awareness he could not leave his apartment for fear of scaring up the neighborhood. For what reason? But still too risky to try. He would have to put all faith in his cat called Compas who looked like a coal-colored animal, Uncle's loyal sentinel. If Compas took a liking to you he would cast a shadow blanket of peace over you. If Compas took a disliking interest he would distort his enemy's appearance with melting images that evoked the canvases of Salvador Dali.

In his younger years Compas had spent what seemed endless weeks in space, wandering in and out of black holes to hide himself. During this time Uncle Bill was blessed with the ability to create inventive realities. Leaving the comfort of Compas's shadow of peace Uncle Bill with optimistic feeling of mental restoration returned to his bedroom mirror. He now understood for the first time what his past life experience all meant. In the scheme of things Uncle Bill felt in his bones a readiness to confront all oncoming obstacles. The loss of facial landscape had given him the cover to launch a whole raft of freshly planned acts of revenge, revenge against those that had crossed him at one time or another.

The first in line was Trevor, or Trev. Uncle Bill Zoom-called Trev, the jumping jerk. "Is that you, Bill? I didn't recognize you without your face." What Uncle Bill did not realize was that Trev was long dead and that the image he evoked was one that he had completely conjured up in his mind. "Trev, my old friend," continued Uncle Bill with a voice that seemed to come from an empty stomach. "I've come to kill you with a garden trowel. You cannot escape, and the police will never find the murder weapon." Uncle Bill cut the call before Trev could respond.

The last image Uncle Bill saw was the face of distilled fear. When Uncle Bill turned in for the night with a look of dissolute comfort on what remained of his face he dreamt he had turned into an enormous dome on legs in the shape of the White House. The mystery was how did he know the dome was a vast version of his impending self?

The dome was headed down the Concourse into a wall of armed and imbedded security police. Uncle Bill once again saw his image in the bathroom mirror. His face was now fully restored. His features were all as he remembered them. An officer gave an order to open fire. The bathroom mirror exploded into a thousand shards. When all the parts were put together and the facts were known Uncle Bill's last facial expression was one that only Compas could comprehend.

The Man's Thoughts

After a text by Hans Arp

I n his head the next thought splits from the previous thought and the following thought splits from the thought before, and like one vast, simple cell structure multiplies rapidly until one day the top of his head is blown clean off, hat and all, leaving his thoughts naked and seeming to look like one stupendous bunch of polished glass grapes.

The ideas that lived in the thoughts of the grapes on the whole felt not in the least discomforted and soon settled down. Some of the older thoughts felt dizzy and a bit tottery, but they were getting on in years and expected some pushing and shoving from the younger, more boisterous ones.

Some of the middle-aged thoughts looked back over their lives and tried to assess, if to some degree of satisfaction, they had made full use of their lives. Most of them felt if they were to live their lives over again they would have done all the same things, made all the same decisions and so forth.

Some of the younger thoughts, the little whippersnappers, as the older ones called them, beheld a surplus of active energy. It was with just cause that the older thoughts worried a lot, and some of them made so bold as to approach the young hot-blooded ones and tell them that if they did not take hold of themselves, they would all topple over and not have a head to stand on. This put the wind up some of the older younger ones and they at least made an effort to contain themselves, showing a good example to the others.

It made little difference, the top of his head being blown off, that is; fresh new thoughts kept piling up under the younger ones. Some of the active thoughts showed concern for the poor, elderly, rickety ones, wobbling about at the top, and felt sure that their little pink glows (their ideas, that is) were lacking a little luster.

In the evening just before sleeping all the thoughts rallied together for a bit of sing-song. It was a good thing and did more to gladden the sad hearts of those not so youthful. It strengthened a sense of comradeship, yes, and love for one's fellow man, and woman. Oh Yes, there were some who still felt this strong love for a member or members of the opposite gender, young or old, it made no difference, the little common souls clung together. Of course this did a lot to raise the singing up, made it sweeter, made it seem worthwhile in a manner of speaking.

The older thoughts took the bass parts except for the ladies. The middle-aged thoughts filled in the contraltos and tenors, and the younger thoughts sung tenor, soprano and anything they could squeeze from their innermost hearts.

The singing was very good, like a big choir of heavenly hosts, because some of the older ones were so far from the ground they would disappear in the cloud sometimes. The music made the man's face happy. You could see him smiling. He liked it.

Some of the younger thoughts often felt troubled by the fact that in bad weather some of the elderly thoughts would come a cropper, be laid up for days with a bad cold or worse still, influenza. It was soon decided though that at such times they should all huddle a little closer together; there was a lot of laughing when they did that.

To get back to the evening concerts, they would go on long into the night; all notions of time completely escaped them. It was like one long, breathless sigh.

One day each thought was given a piece of paper and a felt-tipped pen. They were each to draw whatever took their fancy, to not hold anything back. It was truly amazing because the thoughts had only a ghost-like idea of how the man's face really looked, but they all drew his face quite perfectly; they all drew his face smiling, just like he looks asleep as he hovers between light and darkness.

The Ward's Spare

The morgue is in Stetford
Michelle's in Vermont
Tea taketh me to fly in lean plasters
He speedeth me bestride shrill daughters
Me poureth Lysol
Re-sheaves me in the lightlessness for distains hate
Hey! Though I stalk through the alley of meth
Thy shall spear no weevil
For few are with me
More sod, the more wrath may comport thee
Few compare a fable to bore me in the pretense
   of high energy
You disjoint, they said, and despoil: my butt runs
   in clover
Poor me, foodless and curse-free
Towel hollow thee all the ways of a knife
And I feel swell in the blouse of the morgue whatever

Thirteen Fright Nights of Hallows Eve

On the first night of Hallows Eve
My keeper gave to me
A drowning man out on the sea

On the second night of Hallows Eve
My keeper gave to me
Two ta-tas teasing
And a drowning man out on the sea

On the third night of Hallows Eve
My keeper gave to me
Three fogies wheezing
Two ta-tas teasing
And a drowning man out on the sea

On the fourth night of Hallows Eve
My keeper gave to me
Four sinners sneezing
Three fogies wheezing
Two ta-tas teasing
And a drowning man out on the sea

On the fifth night of Hallows Eve
My keeper gave to me
Five embalmers greasing
Four sinners sneezing
Three fogies wheezing
Two ta-tas teasing
And a drowning man out on the sea

On the sixth night of Hallows Eve
My keeper gave to me
Six sexpots squeezing
Five embalmers greasing

Four sinners sneezing
Three fogies wheezing
Two ta-tas teasing
And a drowning man out on the sea

On the seventh night of Hallows Eve
My keeper gave to me
Seven buttocks breezing
Six sexpots squeezing
Five embalmers greasing
Four sinners sneezing
Three fogies wheezing
Two ta-tas teasing
And a drowning man out on the sea

On the eighth night of Hallows Eve
My keeper gave to me
Eight incubators freezing
Seven buttocks breezing
Six sexpots squeezing
Five embalmers greasing
Four sinners sneezing
Three fogies wheezing
Two ta-tas teasing
And a drowning man out on the sea

On the ninth night of Hallows Eve
My keeper gave to me
Nine corpses leeching
Eight incubators freezing
Seven buttocks breezing
Six sexpots squeezing
Five embalmers greasing
Four sinners sneezing
Three fogies wheezing
Two ta-tas teasing
And a drowning man out on the sea

On the tenth night of Hallows Eve
My keeper gave to me
Ten armpits cheesing
Nine corpses leeching

Eight incubators freezing
Seven buttocks breezing
Six sexpots squeezing
Five embalmers greasing
Four sinners sneezing
Three fogies wheezing
Two ta-tas teasing
And a drowning man out on the sea

On the eleventh night of Hallows Eve
My keeper gave to me
Eleven gonads creeping
Ten armpits cheesing
Nine corpses leaching
Eight incubators freezing
Seven buttocks breezing
Six sexpots squeezing
Five embalmers greasing
Four sinners sneezing
Three fogies wheezing
Two ta-tas teasing
And a drowning man out on the sea

On the twelfth night of Hallows Eve
My keeper gave to me
Twelve testes bleaching
Eleven gonads creeping
Ten armpits cheesing
Nine corpses leaching
Eight incubators freezing
Seven buttocks breezing
Six sexpots squeezing
Five embalmers greasing
Four sinners sneezing
Three fogies wheezing
Two ta-tas teasing
And a drowning man out on the sea

On the thirteenth night of Hallows Eve
My keeper gave to me
Thirteen scalps a-screeching
Twelve testes bleaching

Eleven gonads creeping
Ten armpits cheesing
Nine corpses leaching
Eight incubators freezing
Seven buttocks breezing
Six sexpots squeezing
Five embalmers greasing
Four sinners sneezing
Three fogies wheezing
Two ta-tas teasing
And a drowning man out on the sea

When Ends Justify the Means
(A story told to Gus Gross, Aged Six)

"Once upon a time there was an uncle and a nephew"

"Which was which?"

"Well, the uncle was bigger than the nephew, just like my wife, your Auntie Rhubarb, that is"

"Are uncles always big, then?"

"Yes, they are, if everyone around them stays as small as they are"

"What do you mean?"

"Well, if his family suddenly grew larger, he wouldn't be very big, would he?"

"No, but my Uncle Humbert isn't very big"

"Ah yes, but Uncle Humbert is a microbiologist; he studies very tiny bodies"

"Are people who look at tiny things always small then?"

"Why, of course they are, how otherwise would they be able to look at tiny living things? Anyway, do you want to hear the story or don't you?"

"Sorry"

"Once upon a time there was an uncle and a nephew. The uncle was rich, very rich …"

"How rich?"

"His income was more than adequate, but he also knew lots of politicians and statesmen and had a number of villas in Southern California, also he …"

"And personal bodyguards, did he have personal bodyguards, too?"

"Of course. He had to have personal bodyguards to protect him against people"

"What about big cars, did he have any big cars?"

"Yes, he had 14 armor-plated limousines"

"Were they bullet proof?"

"Oh yes, three of them had a turret on the top and the rest were coated with a silver paint which meant if you looked at the limousine, all you saw was your own reflection"

"Why were the cars silver?"

"Well, that was because every time you looked, you were reminded of how poor you were as compared to him"

"Did he let his nephew ride in any of the silver cars?"

"Do you want to hear the story or don't you?"

"Sorry, I won't interrupt again!"

"But the nephew didn't have any money at all, and that made him very sad"

"Why didn't his uncle give him some?"

"Because all the uncle's money was being spent to make sure he kept everything he already had. Still, the nephew was the old man's sole heir, so …"

""What does *heir* mean?"

"Well, heirs are people who come and get all your money and belongings and everything when you're dead"

"So why didn't the nephew just kill his uncle and take it all?"

"That's a nice thing to ask, I must say! He didn't kill his uncle because you must never, never kill your uncle however much you want to, even to get his belongings"

"Why not?"

"In case the police find out"

"But what if the police don't find out?"

"The police always find out, unless you have lots and lots of money, and besides, if he did not give gifts to his friends, his uncle's friends would tell the police. Anyway, the nephew had a better idea. He'd noticed that his uncle would never allow himself to get upset; he'd never seen his uncle cry at table and fly into a rage when …"

"I bet he was drunk"

"No, he simply went red in the face and held in his anger. He was lachrimalic, you see"

"What does *lachrimalic* mean?"

"Well, it's not very simple to explain. Anyway, I'll try. It's like the blood, you see. Blood is made up of tiny white and red animals, and if, like some poor unfortunate people, you have more of one type of animal than the other, you would bleed to death if you injured yourself and the right kind of help was not at hand"

"Well, the uncle suffered from this same kind of thing, not in his blood, but in his little pouch behind his eyes. This pouch is called the lachrimal sac. This is where tears are made before they run along little tubes into the eyeballs. Now if the uncle became extremely upset and he wept, the tears would flow and never stop until he had drained out all the water in his body, and because the body cannot live without water, he would die. You see, the uncle had more of some chemicals in his pouch than he did of others"

"Will it happen to me?"

"Not if I know you. Anyway, the nephew noticed that what made his uncle extremely unhappy was listening to stories about some of his old statesmen friends who in the past had streaks of bad luck and had lost all of their money. Once he got so upset, he almost died"

"Can you really die weeping?"

"Yes, if you're lachrimalic…. So one day the nephew came to see his uncle just after dinner. The uncle had eaten even more than usual, something that always angered him because he'd suffer bad pains in the stomach as a result of overeating, as you well know"

"Like the Alka-Seltzer commercial on T.V.?"

"Yes, that's right … and so the nephew thought to himself: 'Aha! Now's the time.' And he told him the disastrous story of how a State Governor friend of his uncle's had lost everything he owned when the Federal Government set up a committee to look into his business affairs, the story was so sad that …"

"Tell me the story!"

"Wait a moment, and I'll tell it to you afterwards … anyway, the uncle listened to the story and got so distressed that his whole face became convulsed beneath floods of irrepressible tears. In fact, the whole house was flooded out, and he died, but the nephew of course managed to swim to safety"

"Yes, but what was the story?"

"Wait a minute …. So, after the uncle's funeral, the nephew got everything"

"Even the silver cars?"

"Yes, everything. He was the sole heir, I told you"

"Aunt Rhubarb's very rich. Doesn't she have the same thing wrong with her body?"

"Funny you should ask that, as a matter of fact she …" "Now, will you tell me the story, Uncle?"

"But you know the story … it was the story I've just told you"

"Which one?"

"You know, the one about the uncle and the nephew"

"Will you tell it to me again?"

"Certainly. Once upon a time there was an aunt and a nephew …"

When

1.
When the lightning is stolen by night
And our moon limply falls out of sight

When our islands are swallowed like pills
And the creatures all take to the hills

When our sun breeds a furnace-like keg
And earthquakes split rocks like an egg

When the gods highjack thunder annoyed
And our earthship rolls into a void

When the winds blow the graveyards away
And hurricanes drill holes in the clay

When the rains fall like oceans
Causing astral commotions

When our sleep is swallowed by dreams
And all is not all what it seems

2.
When disease is our master
Who left nothing, just laughter
Don't you wonder where we went astray
When ill health is the norm
Just our deeds keep us warm
Don't you wonder where common sense lay

—Oakland, Ca., August, 2021

Opal & Ellen Nations. *Photograph by Heather Duncan*

ABOUT THE AUTHOR

British-born artist, writer, singer and gospel music producer / researcher Opal Louis Nations was born in Brighton, England in 1941. Close to 600 works of fiction and art have appeared in books and small magazines. One of his earliest texts was published in Michael Moorcock's *New Worlds Magazine* in 1969.

During the 1960s, he backed the early soul band The Frays and recorded for Decca. He also sang in Alexis Korner's short-lived gospel quartet and with the Ram John Holder Group out of London's Marquee Club.

In the mid-1970s, he was awarded both The Perpetua and Pushcart prizes for his fiction and appeared on Yehudi Menhuin's T.V. series *Man And His Music*. During the 1980s and 1990s he hosted a gospel and R&B radio show over Berkeley's KPFA. He has had published at least 40 books of his own experimental fiction and artwork. In more recent times he served as co-producer on Robert Clem's *How They Got Over* shout gospel documentary and appeared on German television Channel 4's program *Soul Power*.

Some of his graphic works reside at the Getty Museum in Los Angeles as part of the Jean Brown Archive. Well over 150 of his music articles covering a wide range of music genres have appeared in music magazines. He has written liner notes to over 130 CD collections. He produced the Legendary Gospel Specialty reissue series for Fantasy Records in Berkeley and the Nashboro Gospel reissue series for AVI in Los Angeles.

Recently, Black Scat published his two music-related books, *Brushes With Music: With Strokes in 1960s British Rock,* and *Sensational Nightingales: The Story of Joseph "Jo Jo" Wallace and the Early Days of the Sensational Nightingales.*

OTHER BLACK SCAT BOOKS YOU'LL ENJOY

THE ALPHONSE ALLAIS READER
Alphonse Allais

NOMINATA
Doug Skinner

SPECULATIONS
Alfred Jarry

COLLECTED MONOLOGUES
Charles Cros

LE CHAT NOIR EXPOSED
Caroline Crépiat

SMELLS LIKE TEEN 'PATAPHYSICS
Norman Conquest

THE COMPLETE UNABRIDGED LEXICON
Opal Louis Nations

THE NEW URGE READER OMNIBUS
various

THE PISSERS' THEATRE
Eckhard Gerdes

THE ART OF NOISES
Luigi Russolo

CRITICS & MY TALKING DOG
Stefan Themerson

THE GRAND EQUATION
Tom Whalen

THE PUPPET-PLAY OF DOCTOR GALL
Jason E. Rolfe

FROM THEIR LIPS TO HIS EAR
Denis Diderot

WEIRDLY OUT WEST
Rhys Hughes

BRANDO BLEEDS
Harold Jaffe

www.ingramcontent.com/pod-product-compliance
Lightning Source LLC
Chambersburg PA
CBHW050830180626
46814CB00004B/1552